VIVA CHRISTO REY!
The Amazing Story of God's Work among the Poor of El Paso-Juarez

To dear Esther,
With much love
in Jesus,
from Lynette.
(6/8/90.)

VIVA CHRISTO REY!

The Amazing Story of God's Work among the Poor of El Paso-Juarez

René Laurentin

WORD PUBLISHING

Word (UK) Ltd
Milton Keynes, England

WORD BOOKS AUSTRALIA
Heathmont, Victoria, Australia
SUNDAY SCHOOL CENTRE WHOLESALE
Salt River, South Africa
ALBY COMMERCIAL ENTERPRISES PTE LTD
Scotts Road, Singapore
CHRISTIAN MARKETING LTD
Auckland, New Zealand
CROSS (HK) CO
Hong Kong
EUNSUNG CORP
Seoul, Korea
PRAISE INC
Quezon City, Philippines

CONTENTS

FOREWARD

This book will probably surprise and possibly shock the average British Christian who reads it. This is not just because it comes from a different culture – the passionate, almost crude catholicism of the Latin American poor – but because it challenges and disturbs some of our most deeply implanted religious attitudes. It is a book that asks us to believe that miracles happen now, that they are verifiable, frequent and lasting, and that they concern not only bodily or mental healing (which most of us can fit into our rational world-view) but things like boxes of grapes and cans of condensed milk.

Its author is a distinguished French theologian, a Roman Catholic priest and an expert in the investigation of miracles. He visited the Rio Grande to follow up persistent reports of miracles occurring in the Christian communities that were flourishing amongst the poor. The book is mostly his own record of what he saw and heard.

The uncommitted or sceptical reader may feel that Fr. René's objectivity has at times deserted him. The Protestant reader may wince occasionally at the kind of catholicism which he does not often meet in Europe – a faith that treads the borders of superstition without a 'proper' sense of caution. But the sheer warmth and humanity and goodness of the story, and its wonderful picture of a Jesus who still has 'good news for the poor' has a conviction all of its own. It is neither easily put down, nor quickly forgotten.

DAVID WINTER (Head of Religious Broadcasting BBC)

A Note to the Reader

On the Rio Grande, along the border between the United States and Mexico, rubbish-combers of Juarez are reliving the gospel at a site called the Dump. The good news proclaimed to the poor is prospering and producing its effect around the garbage and refuse of this Mexican city. There are conversions, the spirit of joy and thankfulness abounds, and self-help projects of various kinds are flourishing. Affluent individuals are selling their possessions and joining the life of the community that has sprung up. Are there also the miracles of the gospel, cures, the multiplication of food? It may seem hard to believe, but such things are said to have happened.

Father René Laurentin is known for his studies of miracles at Lourdes and other places. Servant Publications suggested that he go and ascertain the facts at Juarez. He went, sifted, and has now evaluated. What he discovered was a resurgence of God's marvels, the kind that occurs wherever Jesus Christ is completely accepted.

After reporting his findings, he takes up the question of evaluation, in which he is careful to define the problems faced in any verification of miracles. To this evaluation he brings the illumination that has made him, a leading expositor on the subject. He does not, however, present his own preconceived ideas, but leaves readers to pass their own judgment on the remarkable facts presented.

"Returning today from El Paso," he writes, "I read the gospel with a more familiar eye and understanding. The task I set myself was to search out the facts without exaggerating or minimizing anything and without being either naive or hypercritical. I was not disappointed. The rubbish-combers at the Dump live in vast *barrios* with no running water, no electricity, no regular employment, no public welfare or social security. Yet in spite of this they have formed successful cooperative ventures which they manage themselves. But most importantly, they have found in the Holy Spirit the source of the spiritual conversion that has made for more humane living through converted action. The Holy Spirit, too, has given them a capacity for renewal, a capacity rarely found among intellectuals, who are so often lost in things, in learning, and in the orchestrated power and influence that earned the rich the reproach of Jesus. The gospel is still the good news proclaimed to the poor."

Christmas at the Dump

El Paso, Autumn of 1972—Father Richard Thomas was reading a passage from Luke's gospel to a charismatic prayer group.

> When you give a dinner or a banquet, do not invite your friends or your brothers or your kinsmen or rich neighbours, least they also invite you in return, and you be repaid. But when you give a feast, invite the poor, the maimed, the lame, the blind, and you will be blessed, because they cannot repay you. (14:12–14).

This is a call to us, concluded the group amidst prayer. Accordingly, they decided to share Christmas dinner with the poor of Juarez, on the other side of the Rio Grande. But before this dinner would be possible, the rubbish-combers would have to come to an agreement among themselves, because their very misery had pitted them against each other. A sort of law of the jungle prevailed between the two hostile groups that had formed. Physical blows and injuries, even deaths, had occurred.

A truce was arranged and the dinner took place as scheduled, on Christmas Day (from 11:00 to 4:30). The people who came numbered twice as many as their hosts were prepared to serve, 300 instead of 150. But still there was more than enough food. Everybody received a generous portion of choice ham. After dinner, there was a considerable amount of leftovers, and these were given to the people to take with them.

Since then, it is said, miracles have been happening in Juarez. Conversions are many and their effects are lasting. A communal life has sprung up, which involves common prayer and the sharing of food as at the time of the Acts of the Apostles. The poor have mobilized. They have taken charge of their community. Persons of means have joined them, after selling what they owned. Mexicans and Yankees are working together as brothers and sisters. Holiness is thriving on unlikely soil. Can one also speak of miracles? Everyone must judge for himself, after reading this account of what I heard and saw at El Paso and Juarez in the hot summer sun of July, 1979.

ONE

Impressions from El Paso

Getting off the plane at El Paso on Friday, July 6, 1979, at the end of a long day of thirty-two hours (counting the eight-hour time difference from Paris), I entered a unique world: the world of American civilization, mechanized, computerized, planned and systematized. I made my way through the tunnel-like corridor of the airport, lit as usual with *Exit* signs, and caught sight of a tall figure whom I recognized from a picture. It was Father Richard Thomas, and I was seeing him for the first time. He had come to meet me, dressed in blue jeans that were tucked into tall, half-laced boots. His robust appearance spoke of Irish ancestry with a rich mixture of French Canadian and other influences. His were strong features which occasionally burst into loud laughter, easing an inner tension which he had little trouble controlling by force of character and the grace of God.

With him was a youthful septuagenarian with a short, well-trimmed beard. His name was Bill Halloran, an engineer by profession. His career had been devoted to building bridges. A few months ago he left Rhode Island to join the community at El Paso. Now he was building a different kind of bridge along the border between the United States and Mexico, joining the two contrasting worlds and cultures that I was to find there.

Father Thomas drove the truck himself; it was one of the latest models. He drove steadily, slowly, all of a third under the posted speed, 20 mph where it was 30: the slowness of great accomplishers who know how to make themselves last. His composure tempered my impatience to get to the journey's end, after so many hours of flight, so many takeoffs and landings.

The truck stopped in front of a white, two-storey house with overhanging beams. It was one of the homes of the community, and I found there the warm welcome characteristic of charismatic houses. It was the middle of the night in El Paso but seven in the morning by my inner clock (Paris time). My hosts did not try to keep me up, and I went straight to bed. I had no trouble waking the next morning; it was three o'clock in the afternoon in France. I set my watch. That day, Saturday, without prior arrangement or discussion, we travelled in the same truck for a visit to the other houses of the community.

La Cueva

The first stop was La Cueva (2209 Great Bear Court). This was a centre for the students of a nearby high school. Here at the centre one could see evidence of the tragedies and pains of modern civilization, including the effects of drugs. Fights and injuries were commonplace. One of the students spoke up: "We need some musclemen to keep order here."

Father Thomas, a friend of animals from childhood and never without his dog Ginger, suggested that they try the intelligent Labrador, Fe, who acted as watchdog outside: "Why not bring her inside and see what happens?" The presence of Fe (a Spanish name meaning faith) put an end to violence and disorder like magic. She was immune to the anxiety of the human counsellors, who were constantly fearful of an outburst. Fe was just quietly there, with her instinct. A young man was spotted smoking marijuana. One of the counsellors politely asked him to leave. He refused. Fe threatened him so convincingly that the nervous recalcitrant dashed to safety on top of a car that was parked outside. Another time the dog, smelling an instrument of malice, began to behave agressively toward a perfectly behaved youth: he had a knife concealed in his pocket. The youth lost no time getting rid of it. After fifteen days order was established. No miracle here, just the instinct of an animal and the respect it inspired. That was enough to restore some sanity to human madness.

"I had been looking for a dog who would be friendly to children and at the same time protect the house," Rick told me. "After praying and scouting around, I selected this Labrador named Madge and renamed her Fe." Rick esteems animals, like St. Francis of Assisi. "When the young people raise acclamations to Christ the King, Fe jumps and barks magnificently, giving them an excellent example of praise. Does not scripture say that God is wonderful in his creatures?"

Next we paid a brief visit to a third house (1408 Delta Street): it was in a sad state. The people living here, a nurse and her charges, must have been too preoccupied to worry about orderliness and the relaxed comfort usually found in American homes.

The Centre

Last we came to Our Lady's Youth Centre (OLYC), a large, featureless building whose walls, inside and out, showed no trace of recent paint or scrubbing. It was here that Rick Thomas was assigned, May 31, 1964, to devote himself to social work. It was here that it all began.

Though the structure itself was drab and lacking in aesthetic appeal, the warm reception given to me by its inhabitants impressed me. The centre is staffed by volunteers and conducts various kinds of social projects, including an employment service. It functions smoothly, at the same time maintaining a certain amount of flexibility.

The faces I met there were pleasant and smiling and offered a welcome contrast to the dull pavement of the grounds. Testimonials of simple conviction adorned the walls. Where the gospel is alive, it finds expression.

There was also this "want ad," which defied the conventional promise of a good salary: "If you want to *volunteer* to help us, we can put you to work. Glory to God!"

Our Lady's Youth Centre is simple yet effectively organized. It has become a distribution centre of food for the poor of Juarez, the Mexican city that begins at the end of the street, just a few hundred yards from the centre.

Crossing the Rio Grande

We are now on our way to Juarez.

In one direction, from the United States to Mexico, it takes no time at all to cross the border, without inspection. We were over before I knew it. But there is nothing grand about the Rio Grande, the river that forms a natural boundary between Texas and Mexico. In the 16th and 17th centuries it may have been hundreds of yards wide. But today it has shrunk to thirty or forty feet, at most.

From the Mexican side of the river, people stood looking across to the American side. No doubt some were there just to cool off or to go bathing, in water polluted by the sewage of the city. Others were waiting for a chance to get across, to add to the millions of clandestine Hispanics in quest of work in the United States.

The transition from El Paso to Juarez is enormous. But language is no longer the most common hurdle. Many Americans speak Spanish in El Paso, and many Mexicans speak English in Juarez. But the break in culture is deep and abrupt. It is the stark contrast between a world that is rich, organized, and powerful and a world that is poor and disorganized, where everything seems left to chance or improvisation. Instead of modern roads and streets running at right angles, systematically marked and provided with stop signs and signal lights that are respected, what I found was more like a labyrinthine puzzle.

We drove along the Rio Grande for just a few minutes and then turned onto an "auto route," so named because it was restricted to automobile traffic. Actually, it was an ordinary dirt road with two lanes that ran over a dried-up river bed. I would not recommend it in a downpour. But, fortunately, downpours are rare in these parts. On leaving this zigzag river road and coming into the open, what I saw was staggering: a vast wasteland crowded with wretched dwellings— paperboard shacks many of them, others made of salvaged tin or metal. Rain collapses the paperboard, and the sun makes an oven of the tin and metal shacks.

In this immense barrio live 200,000 people, one fourth of the population of Juarez. From the air, El Paso and Juarez looks like one large city with no perceptible demarcation by the Rio Grande. But the reality is far different. On the one side is the methodical layout, evidence of American norms and enterprise; on the other is a sort of chaos, from the centre of which rises a monument to material wealth, a cluster of tall modern buildings with their neon lights, while all about, misery sprawls and covers an area miles square.

There is nothing "livable" about the barrio: no electricity, no city water, no sanitation. Outside each home stand metal barrels for water. Ancient tank trucks, rusted and dust-covered, fill the barrels for twenty pesos (about a dollar). The trucks leave as they come, raising an enormous cloud of dust in the sandy, trackless ground. Peering over these metal barrels containing stale and sometimes fetid water, the heart sinks. Is this really what they use, not only for washing and cooking but for drinking!

No Work, No Social Security, No Urban Living

Homes, such as they are, defy the steep hills. They stretch as far up as water can be delivered, and sometimes farther, in which case people come down the hill, fill their containers from the nearest barrel and clamber back up. The shining sun and an occasional stand of shrub are the only redeeming touches on this desolate landscape. But sand and desert notwithstanding, people abound and take life in their stride. Children are generally attractive, bright-eyed and with a ready smile. Even bare-headed, as they usually are, they seem to take to the sun at its hottest without the least discomfort. Despite impossible living conditions, these Mexican people have lost none of their fine qualities. Wherever we went, we found them all smiles, happy to see us.

Carlotta's face beamed as she invited us to visit her home, an adobe structure of two rooms, just recently built for her large family of seven children, the youngest a few months old. This house, what a difference! It was simple yet functional and had been built by the Christian community that was established here. These walls were not paperboard but solid masonry capped by strong, protective roofing. It was a relief to go inside and, instead of an oven, find escape from the heat.

"It's a palace!" exclaimed Carlotta. It could be kept up. Cleanliness was possible. A wonder.

But there was a much deeper wonder in her life: a conversion and a cure. "Before, I was *sucia del corazon del cuerpo*" (unclean in heart and body), Carlotta told us.

The uncleanness of heart and body had disappeared along with the squalor of the hole she had lived in. Carlotta's uncleanness had been very real in another sense. Her doctor had told her that she had uterine cancer. Anticipating an operation, she really felt sick. The community began to pray for her, and she began to get well.

"No operation, no doctor!" exclaimed Carlotta.

Not long after, she gave birth to a beautiful Mexican baby, now six to seven months old. *Gracias a Dios!*

Thankfulness likes simple words that rekindle joy.

Emerging from Carlotta's house I noticed another

revolution. Instead of metal barrels containing rancid water, there was a large concrete container with a cover and a spigot at the base. The water was protected and the container could be kept clean. Here was real progress. I suppose I ran a great risk taking a drink from this water, but here the people are proof against much worse.

In a nearby house we found Misael Luis Gonzalez Sanchez, a handsome young Mexican, already father of a fairly large family—two boys and two girls. On a wall, in his own hand, were the words: "God is our refuge and strength, an ever-present help in distress." I recognized the beginning of Psalm 46.

"That's so we don't forget we have a Saviour," he explained.

His hands and face were both excited. Even his hair seemed to smile. Black and naturally curly. It was styled as the Renaissance painters would have loved. The words of the psalmist 3,000 years ago assumed new life and meaning in Misael's experience: a total conversion, about which he told me.

I was born in Michoacan and at twelve went to Mexico City. I had a hard time there. I slept in the streets or wherever I could find a place. I worked when there was work, mostly on errands or repairing bicycles. But most of the time there was no work. After military service, I met my wife Ana. I began to work in construction but spent the money on drink. As a result we were destitute. I had given my wife three children but took little or no care of my family.

It was then that we left for Juarez. Like so many others, I decided to cross the Rio Grande secretly to find well-paid work on the other side. I succeeded in crossing over and found a job as a roofer. But I couldn't cross the river until four in the morning, and if I wanted to come back I had to do it late at night, to elude the patrol. I made more money but much of it again went to drink. My wife had to go trash digging to provide for the family.

One night I was chased by the patrol. In the chase I tripped over a wire and was badly hurt. They took me to a hospital. I had a dislocated shoulder and a broken collarbone. It was so bad that the officer took me to a hospital in El Paso. When I came home from the hospital, I found my situation had worsened. We were now six, my wife and I had another child. We lived in a five- by eight-foot paperboard shack. Often we had nothing to eat. At first the neighbours helped us. But things kept getting worse. There was no more they could do. My youngest child, a boy of one year, suffered from fever and constant diarrhoea. I wasn't well, either, what with vomiting and the pain in my shoulder and collarbone. I thought I was in my last days, and I was angry with God. I didn't want anyone to speak about him to my children. I said he did not exist.

It was at this time that my wife learned of the Lord's Food Bank. There she found help. These people asked me if I wanted them to pray for me. I was so sick that I said yes. I began to feel better but not yet well. Again I was taken to the hospital. The people at the Food Bank also prayed for my little son. But the child died. I was heartsick, but I understood that nothing happens without God's will. At his death I gathered my wife and children and we knelt around the child and thanked God for everything. It was a little while yet before I could go to work at the Food Bank. But that did not prevent the people there from helping me and finding me a new place to live.

I was asked to come to a healing session. I went, because my collarbone was not yet healed, and I had a doctor's appointment coming up. They prayed for me at the healing session. A young woman there had a vision in which she saw the broken bone healed. I was sceptical.

That was Monday, and my appointment with the doctor was Wednesday.

"Should I go to El Paso?" I asked.

"Save yourself the trouble, you are healed. Have confidence," they said to me.

I did go back to the hospital, and I thank God because, since that day, I am well. I felt so well that I decided to go back to work in El Paso. I left the Food Bank and resumed my illegal work. Before long, however, I came down with advanced tuberculosis. There was to be no contact with my family. All my clothes were to be burned. But the hospital refused me admission for fear of contagion. The only thing left was treatment by a doctor. Hardly anyone thought I would live. My only choice was to return home. The members of the community prayed regularly for me. After a while I went back to the hospital. They took X-rays, which showed that all trace of the tuberculosis was gone. I was in good health again and was able to return to work at the Food Bank. I understood that the Lord heals and that he had managed everything.

Since then we have received many blessings. Life with my wife and children is completely changed. I used to beat them. Now I love them. They have always loved me. It was I who neglected them. Now we pray together and ask the Lord to give us wisdom and understanding. If you only knew how surprised they were, my wife and children, who had seen me drowned in alcoholism.

I looked again at the wall on which Misael had traced these words: "God is our refuge and strength, an ever-present help in distress" (Ps 46:1). He wasn't likely to forget that he had a Saviuor.

On a table were some imitation flowers. Against the wall stood a guitar and violin. In a corner were lots of small batteries. "Do you sell these?" "No," he replied, "they're for my cassettes." He showed me his collection. What were they about? Without exception, they concerned the word of God and testimonials of healing.

The Dump

From Misael's house we went to the famous Dump: receiving ground for the city refuse, where the story of these communities began, December 25, 1972, at eleven in the morning.

The Dump is always there. Trucks disgorge the rubbish collected in the city, dumping it on, layer after layer, to a depth of twenty feet or more: iron scraps, pots and pans, rags, and nondescript articles of every conceivable sort. But it is not a jungle. The rubbish-combers now form a cooperative, which they manage themselves. Management is head-quartered in a building in downtown Juarez, which we shall visit later. At the Dump, at high noon, the people introduced to me told of other conversions and wonders. Several of them had witnessed the multiplication of food, Frank Alarcon in particular.

Manuel Mendez had been cured of tuberculosis. "They found me lying on my bed," he related. "I was coughing blood, which the chickens came and fed on. Prayers were offered for me, and very soon I was back on my feet, my health restored."

At another time, still fresh in everyone's mind, a truck carrying flammable liquid caught fire at the Dump. The entire community rushed to the scene and called upon the name of the Lord. Three times they prayed in his Name, with all their fervour, and each time the flames quickly subsided.

In March, 1973, a school teacher by the name of Irma Padilla had tried to teach reading to some children of the community who had been undernourished from infancy. Their attention span was practically nil, a minute or two at best. First she tried the picture method, then the phonetic method, using words she thought would interest them. But it was all in vain. In three months they had not even learned as much as the vowels. She sought the advice of specialists.

Malnutrition, beginning in pregnancy, had produced irreversible effects through lack of protein. So the specialists concluded.

Mrs. Padilla stopped trying. But about the same time, prayers were offered for the children in the course of a prayer meeting, and lo and behold, they began to scribble on the dust-covered automobiles at the Dump. The taste and capacity for learning had come to them. Since this healing, they have succcessfully completed their schooling.

On one of the first days after the famous Christmas dinner, a group prayed for a small girl whose foot and hand had been paralyzed from birth. After about twenty minutes of prayer she regained the use of both hand and foot. But she still could not walk. She was too weak from malnutrition. This became all too evident on visiting the family, whose poverty was tragic. There was no food, not even a scrap in the house. Father Rick and some others brought them some groceries, and the next time they saw the child she was walking.

Here again, as was pointed out to me, God did not act as a bypass for available human means.

All this may seem a little dubious, hearsay rather than substantiated fact. After all, there was no certification, there were no documents to prove a cure. But at that time the members of the community were too poor to have gone to a doctor, whose records might show the existence of a condition, its progress and possibly its cure.

"Proofs of the miraculous you will find only for the rich: there never are any as regards the poor," Rick Thomas observed.

Some days later, before he left me, Rick was going through his files. To his surprise he came upon four snapshots of the child who could not walk, taken the very day of the cure. In one she is seen helpless in her mother's arms, in two others, as she was while the community prayed. The fourth caught her first steps.

We talked some more at the Dump. I used the occasion to take pictures. The young Mexicans were very cooperative. All of them wanted their pictures snapped. They were disappointed that the pictures could not be developed on the spot.

The hot July sun was beating down, and I for one was beginning to wilt. A member of the cooperative took note and kindly brought us out of this "ordeal by fire." He lived nearby. His name was Sergio Conde Varela. His wife's name was Lucia. Their house was comfortable and thickly carpeted. Father Thomas, who had seemed indefatigable, stretched out on the floor. Apparently, the withering sun had taken its toll on him too. I followed his example.

Drawn blinds lent coolness to the house, which was tastefully furnished in fine Mexican decor. We dozed off until we were awakened by the sound of soft music. The master of the house, Sergio, who was about thirty years old, was at the electric organ. He began to sing in Spanish. He played and sang as the Spirit moved, in spontaneous praise to the Lord, and was quickly joined by six or seven other men and women. Two of them had their inseparable guitars. Simple, joyous songs to Christ followed in succession. It was the popular, charismatic repertoire. I should have transcribed the melodies. Hands raised high, in rhythmic clap, Lucia, mistress of the house, took up her tambourine. The celebration lasted a good hour. After that, she offered us refreshments.

Sergio, who now directs the community supply store, told me his story. An economist and lawyer who still teaches classes in finance in Juarez, Sergio was collector of revenue in 1973, when he inspected the supply store. It was his first contact with the Dump, and he prided himself on finding its people in default.

At that time I was a Freemason, I had a position with the local government. I was well-off, but still I was looking for the truth without knowing where to find it. My wife was too. One day we went to a priest for help. Not much came of it except that he recommended a library where I would find some books on religion. This didn't seem very stimulating, but I went anyway and found a book on charismatic renewal. I read it off and on during the next eight months. During that time I inspected the Dump.

I was curious, as the collector of revenue. One of the grubbers I questioned told me that he earned a peso and a half daily. With six children, how could he live? I inspected the supply store that I now direct. It was paying no taxes. That looked suspicious. I called for a meeting of the leaders of the community. They came the following Monday. I spoke with them for two hours. My aim was to find out who or what lay at fault and to assess the proper penalties.

Their talk was a revelation to me. Then there was their prayer. One day I was back there. They prayed in tongues.[1] On the following week our conversation was more cordial. I prayed with them. For a whole year they prayed for my interior healing. The change in me was gradual and deep. We felt the need, my wife and I, of coming regularly to this prayer group. It was there that we met Guillermina, until recently an atheist, and Rick Thomas. Conversion took hold of us,[2] and with it I experienced the need to give up everything: freemasonry, the government, the taxes, my functions as a lawyer. It was hard, but I found support in what I heard Rick Thomas preach: *To leave all for Christ*.

I sold my possessions and gave away the proceeds. I kept this house because for legal reasons I could not sell it.

I had only three dollars left, which I put into the collection basket at Mass. On that day we were down to zero, happy, though a little uneasy when we thought of tomorrow. I prayed on awaking the next morning, trusting to God's grace.

Meanwhile, a friend who had worked with me in the local government came for a visit. He had learned that the federal government owed me 53,000 pesos. The money came just in time to take care of some problems. Our accounts here are in order. We do a lot of driving for the community. I don't know why, but our gasoline lasts much longer than it used to—two or three weeks instead of one.

"What do you live on?" I asked.

"I still teach technical courses (on finance and fiscal policy). But my interests have completely changed. The life of faith, it is a beautiful life. *Es muy bonita la vida de fe.*"

There was no need for him to also say, "I am happy." His Mexican smile said it, from the moment I met him at the Dump to the time he played and sang at the organ. His parting smile as I left him at the end of his story was especially radiant.

What a pity that one cannot do everything at once: mingle and talk with people, take notes, snap pictures. Sergio is indeed a beautiful person, dark-skinned, tall, and handsome. He seems to have every talent: a gift for words, for retelling things, for music and song. He radiates a happiness that was reflected in the smile of his wife as she sat opposite him on the carpet.

The Lord's Ranch

The sun was more tolerable as we set out on the way back to the United States. Crossing from the Mexican side was more difficult than our crossover to Juarez had been that morning. Hundreds of cars and trucks were waiting in line, four abreast. Crossings are checked carefully because of clandestine immigration.

We made a stop at OLYC (Our Lady's Youth Centre) to pick up provisions and to freshen up. Then we headed west, to the Lord's Ranch, thirty-three miles from El Paso. Along either side of the highway lay a sandy, desert-like plain extending as far as the eye could see, to the first signs of the Rocky Mountains in the distance. I wondered what sort of oasis the ranch where we were going could be. Near Vado, New Mexico we turned right onto a dirt road that had been opened expressly to serve the ranch. It was a winding, sandy road with sharp ups and downs, and the experience of driving over it was much like riding a toboggan. I appreciated Rick Thomas' slow, steady driving on this bumpy ride.

The ranch was born of a dream, in 1974. That summer the Youth Centre had given up its vacation camp. Another had to be found. The dream became a reality on December 23, 1974, when eighty acres of this desert wilderness were acquired. The soil is not bad, but unproductive for lack of water. One of the first attempts to find water was made on the Lord's Ranch. Rick consulted an expert, who recommended that he dig two wells. The capacity of the two 600-foot-deep wells proved enormous: 1,000 gallons each per minute. Ever since, young people on vacation and parents and even grandparents on weekends have been coming to clear brush, plant trees and shrubs, pull weeds, and do various kinds of work on the Ranch.

The two residences where these temporary volunteers are housed loomed on the horizon and grew progressively larger as we approached. They were good-sized buildings of simple design, with 45-degree roofs shaped to allow for three stories in front and one in the back, at ground level. On each of the two roofs appeared what looked like a small observation tower. No doubt these were for surveillance, which might be necessary on a property that embraces almost a square mile.

At the entrance the sign *The Lord's Ranch* sets the tone. Found on the water storage tank of the ranch are these messages, a reinforcement of the entrance sign:

> You shall love the Lord your God with all your heart, and with all your soul, and with all your mind. This is the greatest and first commandment. And the second is like it. You shall love your neighbour as yourself. (Mt 22: 37–39)

> If any one will not work, let him not eat. (2 Thess. 3:10)

Within the grounds, the roadway, still of sand and dirt, was lined with 3,000 young vines on one side and with trees on the other. Vines and trees were in perfect rows and perfect trim.

On a first tour of the part actually under cultivation (ten percent of the square mile), I estimated about 1,000 fruit trees, which were beginning to produce different kinds of apples, pears, peaches, prunes, and figs (300 of these were fig trees). Other trees have been planted around three artificial ponds which together cover about seven acres. As well as acting as a windbreak, these trees will provide shade and beauty in the future.

The ranch raises catfish, a good source of protein. They are fed meat too tough for human consumption, but which they have no trouble tearing apart. Two young women with large knives were struggling to cut up some of this raw meat. The pieces tossed into the pond spangled with their blood-red colour. The fish seemed to take little notice at first. But after I returned from a brief walk among the trees, not a trace was left. The meat had disappeared in less time than it took to carve it up.

Work on the ranch, largely dependent on a fluctuating

and inexperienced workforce, is directed by volunteers who themselves have not attended agricultural school. Nevertheless, though the work is often accomplished by improvised methods, the land is carefully and intelligently used. Rows are straight and properly spaced. Ditches have been dug to carry irrigation water. And fruit trees thrive.

It has all been well thought out, and progress is the more remarkable because the means to accomplish it are generally unsophisticated and of the do-it-yourself variety.

Beehives, twenty-six of them, keep up a steady buzz, and 200,000 earthworms have been introduced into the soil, which had lain uncultivated. Four dogs have been trained to scatter rabbits. Too many rabbits means much damage to vines and orchards. In the middle of the ranch are pens for horses, cows, donkeys, goats, and other animals.

Everything produced here will go to feed the impoverished quarters of Juarez. As of now, it is only a beginning.

Work is completely gratis for temporary volunteers. As for full-time workers, they are given room and board. I was asked if such a system would be possible in France, where even the members of religious orders are now enrolled in social security and must make regular contributions to the programme.

At the end of the day everybody returned to the central building, some thirty young men and women in shorts or blue jeans. It had been a hot day, but not unusually hot. Those who worked nearby walked back, but those farther away rode in a truck.

At the centre they found a self-serve meal prepared by Sister Mary Virginia, a St. Vincent de Paul sister who had found the full meaning of her vocation in this movement designed to help the poor. Large, solid, calm, like the *turris davidica* of scripture, she could get a lot done without raising a storm. Her presence was discreet, like that of a mother. I learned that this matters here, given the varied profile of these generally quiet and congenial young people.

Some came from far away. Others had been in trouble; they had had suicidal tendencies, gotten involved with drugs, or had some other problem, though one would not suspect it from their pleasant, undisturbed appearance. As I observed them, I could not tell which of them were there to find themselves, and which were there because they were impelled by pure generosity, sacrificing their vacation to perform toilsome work for the hungering.

The hall where they gathered and ate was plain and only moderately large, about forty feet long and twenty or more wide. All the food was on one table. They helped themselves and ate, most of them sitting on a bench that ran along three sides of the room. If the hall was lacklustre, outside the setting sun shining through the large windows was glorious, a brilliant red sun that contrasted sharply with the dark clouds and made a spectacle of colour so near and real, it seemed, that one might reach out to touch it.

A community spirit prevailed, a joyful spirit, brotherly and loving, the kind that soothes hidden wounds. There was much dancing and singing on return from work, both before and after supper. This evening there was a Mass, as priests were at hand.

"These young people, the quality of their prayer is wonderful," a teaching Brother from New York said to me. He too was on vacation and had come to share the life and work.

Prayer and praise rose spontaneously as Mass was about to begin. Everyone broke into song without cue and formed a procession that went around the interior of the hall and then outside. Brief thunder but with little or no rain had cooled the air just a trifle. Mass began outside. We sat on the ground for the readings and homily.

Yes, indeed, the quality of their prayer gets through to one. It is the prayer that might be experienced in a very fervent monastery, where there is much recollection and interiorness. Humour spiced the homily and evoked easy laughter. The very attention of the audience was a spur to the homilist; a visiting priest who rose to the occasion. But there was neither false exaltation nor spiritual tension. These young people had found the source. It flows of itself. The Mass is both carried by the community and is carrier of the community that occurs in the Eucharist.

Practically every human type was represented among these thirty participants at Mass. They included two or three blacks, half blacks, and Hispanics of varying Indian lineage much seen in the Southwest of the U.S. In addition, there were many blue-eyed, blonde-haired individuals, like the two strapping, young men, obviously the intellectual type, who, though slightly hunched, towered over the group at six-foot-seven. Social backgrounds were similarly mixed, from the most ordinary to the most refined. It showed in their hairstyle, their facial expression, and so on. Some wore expensive clothes, while others dressed simply. There were strong, solidly built individuals and frail-looking souls whom I couldn't imagine working in the field, like the petite blonde with very high dimples, smiling and made to smile, a beautiful flower in the house. With two or three exceptions, their ages ranged from fourteen to twenty-five.

The kiss of peace between the men and women was heart-felt and without innuendo, as between brother and sister. A young woman climbed onto a chair when one of the two giants approached. He smiled graciously: she half teasing, he pleasantly embarrassed.

I was surprised at the way this dissimilar group got along together, and prayed together.

After Communion there was a common thanksgiving, here and there welling forth in charismatic praise. Sister Virginia had remained at her workplace, behind the counter on which were arranged the plates for dinner. Calm as ever, she launched into prophetic utterance: words inspired by the Lord for the benefit of the group, whom she knew well.

Judging from the attention of the listeners, the words met with obvious approval, no matter that she spoke rather at length.

Mass ended as it had begun, on a note of joy. It had lasted all of two hours. It was time to climb the stairs that led to the dormitories. It was a straight stairway with large steps. The dormitory to the left was the women's, to the right the men's, furnished with twenty or more beds in a row. I was given one at the end of the row, a plain, wrought-iron bed, nothing fancy, but it did have a pillow and blanket, the latter quite unnecessary in the withering heat we were having. The others in the dormitory, who slept there regularly, took steps to get the air circulating, but the draft was so strong that it took me a while to get used to it. Sleep was slow in coming and I lay awake half the night, which turned out to be shorter than I expected.

It was not yet four in the morning when I heard the clatter of pots and pans down below. I went to look. It was Sister Mary Virginia. She was already up and getting breakfast.

At five o'clock the lights went on. It was time for early rising, as farmers do everywhere. The freshness of the morning hours is priceless. Breakfast was ready, generous as usual and without fuss. It consisted of eggs with toast.

At six o'clock that Sunday morning we left to go into the field. Rick Thomas brought along three dogs to give them practice at chasing rabbits, creatures that had done considerable damage to the fields. When we came to an area where Rick suspected the rabbits were, he would call the dogs on like an expert. He also used the occasion to inspect the domain.

We went by the animal pens. A dark-haired girl, not very tall but trim and wiry, was milking goats. A young, black man was cleaning the pen.

Same thing for the cows. Horses and donkeys were less work. I saw nobody riding them. I suspect there wasn't time for that.

Another group was watering the young trees planted around the three ponds. One of the ponds had been drained because it was grown over with algae. To empty it was the only way to restore the pond.

Other people were picking fruit. It was the apricot season. Very soon it would be time for apples. The great variety of fruit trees made it possible to space out production over several months until the fall apples, which would keep until the following year, were ripe.

A young lady, perched ten feet above the ground, was steering a huge tractor between rows of young trees. She handled her job like a pro.

Some were working on irrigation, moving the water pipes as needed.

Two groups of four each were cultivating and pulling weeds. One of these groups included the blonde with the dimples; she had pitched in like a farmhand and seemed perfectly at home. She had not lost her smile. Everywhere, I found these young people quietly at work, ready to help one another. Their mood was pleasant and relaxed and so was their attitude toward us. When I took pictures of them, they showed no sign of apprehension or over-eagerness, though some showed just a hint of distrust. It was obvious that they were where they wanted to be at the moment.

At ten o'clock the heat was overwhelming. By eleven, work halted. It was time for lunch and a siesta, followed ordinarily by a Bible session, that is, prayerful study of the word of God. The fruits of these sessions are evident. Today, however, there was Mass instead.

During the thanksgiving Sister Mary Virginia again found inspiration to impart to the community in the name of the Lord. The same air of joy and interiority was evident. Prayer is integrated with the community life and contributes to its integration.

At four o'clock in the afternoon the temperature was more than 100 degrees fahrenheit (112, I was told). It was time for the workers to go back into the field, where they would remain until seven. But in the meantime they had taken a dip in the pool. Living quarters here do not have much room for privacy and seclusion, where one might do some reading or pursue personal interests. But there is a pool on the ranch, near one of the deep wells. The area rimming the pool was blistering hot, too hot for bare feet, I know because I tried it, to my instant regret and retreat.

I was enjoying my stay here, but feeling a little exhausted. Two other visitors who had arrived with me said the same thing. I suggested that we might return to El Paso. Chances for a good night's rest would be better. But the truck wouldn't start. How were we going to get back? Rick Thomas wasn't sure. Time would tell.

And tell it did. In the hours that followed, I ran across Bill Halloran, the ex-bridgebuilder who drove us back in the red pickup used for hauling things. Reassured, I prepared for bed, counting on a sleepful night.

Prayer and Bread at Juarez

At a quarter after six the next morning there was a knock on the door. It was Sister Linda. She came to call me. I had not known when we would be leaving that Monday morning. She was kind enough to prepare breakfast for me while I dressed in haste. In fifteen minutes, so early in the morning, we were at OLYC.

At seven o'clock, having crossed the border, we were back in the wasteland of the first day, not the Dump but the sandy hill quarter where random shacks and improbable dwellings crowded the landscape as far as the eye could see. The community building stood opposite Carlotta's house. To the left, as you entered, was the supply room, and to the right another room measuring about 20×30 feet which served a multiple purpose. It was a chapel, gathering place,

The Dump, the immense trash collector for Mexico's fourth largest city.

Rick Thomas.

3

The Rio Grande. Waste water from El Paso doesn't discourage bathers.

4

Carlotta. The Lord has re-created all things: unity, health, and happiness, in the house built by everyone.

Misael with his wife and children: another healed and happy family in the underprivileged zone of Juarez.

The Dump. Today, smiling faces light up the mountain of trash.

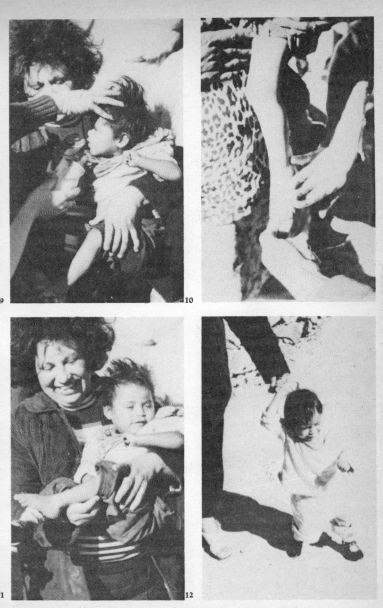

These amateur photos were taken by chance when the foot of the child who was healed was being examined and when she began to walk. Rick was surprised to find them when we were leafing through his loose collection of photos.

Sergio. The joy of new life after he had sold all his belongings.

The Lord's Ranch provides a working vacation for students motivated by the love of God.

Noah and Ezekiel, the two solar-heated homes on the Lord's Ranch.

The students working at the Lord's Ranch share the same prayer, the same joy, and the same source as do the trash grubbers at the Dump.

The Lord's Ranch. A student turned farmer.

Feeding the fish in the desert pond.

The Lord's Ranch. Impeccable rows of fruit trees.

Morning prayer in Juarez. Bible reading and guitar playing give way to deep silence.

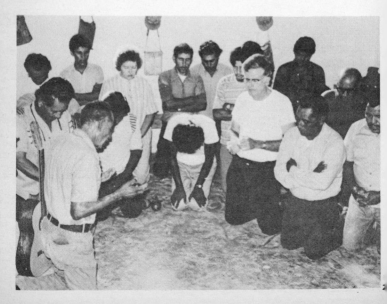

Bible study is an essential part of the life.

Tomás. Farewell to cantinas and crime; joy and health have been regained.

The president of SOCOSEMA (Center), a trash picker elected by the others. To his right, the secretary-general, Guillermina.

Sister Virginia and Rick at the Lord's Ranch, exchanging notes and ideas.

The bishop of Juarez with Guillermina, Rick, and Sister Linda, at the end of our working meeting.

7

Juarez. After everyone prays, everyone works.

On the hill of the future "city," this desert will blossom and become livable.

Mass at the Lord's Food Bank, before work and distribution.

On this desert plateau, Rick plans the "city" of the future.

Juarez. The oil drums of stagnant water are now used for garbage.

Food Bank. Distribution proceeds at a good pace.

and classroom for teaching the rudiments of reading. These people were learning to read. They were motivated by a great desire to be able to read the word of God. Daily prayer had just begun, praiseful prayer, impromptu and self-sustained. It was praise for the daily marvels that God wrought, in the life of each person and in the life of the entire community.

Those who had learned to read held Bibles that were worn along the edges from being thumbed by hands more used to heavy work than to books. The first reading was assigned, the others were left to individual inspiration. Yet there was no overlapping or confusion. Vertical communication with God is best when articulated with the horizontal. Improvised prayers of praise twined with prophecies, with words that one or the other felt impelled to address to the community in the name of the Lord. Anyone unfamiliar with this form of communication might wonder about the pretension or even the lunacy of a person coming forth and saying very simply. "My children, I am with you, count on my love. . . ." But it was nothing more nor less than the direct language of the prophets of Israel, who spoke in straightforward manner unencumbered by rhetoric.

Toward the entrance a man was speaking. He stood half obscured, facing the light. He spoke fluently and with telling gestures. The subject was marriage. I took down some parts:

The union of man and wife is a great thing when one walks in the power of the Lord. The purpose of this union of man and wife is not just pleasure. It allows us to walk with God in marriage. With the power of the Holy Spirit, it is a great blessing. God becomes involved in our human relations: sex, friendship, and the rest. I married my wife to live God's plan of happiness. Outside, there was temptation [he gives a flip of his right hand]. In the name of our Lord Jesus Christ! The Holy Spirit works in us, and in our marriage. . . . All the advice we get about marriage! "Give neither all your money nor all your love to your wife." People say that who don't know the love of God, and the pardon of God. Let us honour God's blessing on our marriage. Glory to God! When we pray together, Christ is there. He takes his place at the centre of everything: the centre of the family, of work. If we get off on the wrong track, we have no excuse. We have a heart [his right hand taps his forehead]. We are not idiots, thanks be to God. So, let us work with God like people of sense.

Applause followed. I began to recognize the speaker. His profile looked familiar, shadowed as it was. It was Sergio Conde, unmistakably. After Sergio had finished, exclamations, prophecies, and readings continued in endless round, and when they were concluded it was without any sign or word or intervention by Father Thomas. The prayer celebration was articulated from within, by a communal inspiration.

Thomas was a solid, broad-shouldered Mexican, a little rotund but muscular. His sparkling eyes lit up the dark complexion of his Mexican face as he related his story:

In 1977, I was sick. That was two years ago. I had very painful arthritis, diabetes, and acute tuberculosis, all at the same time. I just dragged myself along from day to day. Then one day a friend said to me: "*Vamos al banco*", Let's go to the Bank.
"What bank?" I asked.
"The Lord's Bank."
"Are you out of your mind?"
In the end I went with him. I attended Mass. Next morning I went to prayer [like the prayer today, at seven o'clock]. They prayed for my cure. After fifteen days one morning, I got up feeling very energetic and happy [*con*

mucha fuerza y con mucho gusto]. I drank some Coca Cola [forbidden to diabetics] and ate some cake [also forbidden]. But I experienced no ill effects.

That is how I came to join the community.

I asked how old he was. "Sixty-two," he said. I couldn't get over it, his hair was still so black, his vitality so youthful.

I talked with Concepcion Mendoza. Concepcion is a name given to both men and women in Spanish-speaking countries in honor of the Immaculate Conception of Mary. Concepcion was 54 years old, the father of eight children. He told me the following:

Not very long ago I was in charge of fourteen cantinas.

At first I thought he meant common eating places, the French meaning of the word. Actually, *cantina* is a saloon that often camouflages a house of prostitution. That was the case here.

One day Sister Gloria spoke to me of Christ and invited me to come and join in the community prayer.

"Oh, no, I have work to do," I told her.

The end of the workday for me was 4:00. But at 3:15 I felt like leaving. I went to Mass, where they sang with much joy and inspiration. I asked myself: what religion are these people. I am Catholic and won't be anything else.

Mexican Catholicism is deeply ingrained. It has the resistance of certain spores to natural disasters. Its defense seems to harden under persecution or invasion by sectarian groups, which have made much less inroad in Mexico than elsewhere in Latin America.

The charismatic renewal arouses suspicion because its forms of prayers are not the traditional ones. Is it a new

American sect? some ask. Concepcion went on:

> I learned that the community was in the Catholic
> Church. I was very glad to hear that and went back
> home. After that I gave up my cantinas. And now, I am
> working in the community. I am happy to serve God. If
> you ask me, it's the best thing in the world. I am not
> making the money I made before. I made quite a lot, but
> money does not interest me. I am not in want. The few
> things I need I have.

As often happens in situations like this, a backlash
occurred when Concepcion quit the "organization" and
straightened out his life. A false accusation was made
against him to the police, perhaps as an attempt to scare him
or to get even. Just the same, he was arrested and sentenced
to thirteen years in prison. The "initiation" was frightful:
electric shocks, beatings, his head held under water till he
lost consciousness. He still had the scars months later,
which he showed me.

"During these tortures I thought of Jesus Christ. On the
ninth day the accusation was found to be false and I was
freed."

At this point Father Thomas intervened. "This is not the
place to talk about that," he said. "Here I work to change
hearts, not to denounce abuses, when they exist. Our way is
conversion and collaboration with people of good will,
whether poor or of the ruling circles, not confrontation. We
do not make difficulties for ourselves."

Father Thomas' attitude may offend a political
Christianity, which gives priority to denouncing injustice.
But the apostle Paul followed the same course, changing
hearts, not institutions (not even slavery).

Paul counted on his converts to change institutions, not
by demolishing them but by rising above them and trans-
forming them. For his part, he preached submission of

Christians to governments, even to ones that persecuted them, and submission of wives to husbands and of slaves to masters. He sent back Philemon's fugitive slave, whom Paul had baptized, but asked that Philemon receive him as a brother. Philemon did just that, and freed the converted slave.

The Cooperative and Self-Administration

The morning wore on. We left for the urbanized quarters of Juarez, where we stopped in front of a large white building, all one story. It was a comfortable establishment surrounded by a well-kept lawn, American style. This was the home of SOCOSEMA (Sociedad Cooperativ de Seleccion adores de Materiales): The Cooperative Association of Materials Handlers. The handlers were the same refuse diggers we have met before. They assumed this title when they banded together as a community to promote their salvage business. The property itself was on loan to the people of the Basurero (the Dump), who organized into a cooperative with this somewhat more distinguished name.

The building comprised a large gathering hall, some offices, and a workshop where light red dolls were made: heaps of arms, legs, and blonde wigs waiting to be put together, with faces still more fair than the rest of the assemblage.

In one of the offices I met Guillermina Villalva, secretary-general and the moving force behind the whole enterprise from the beginning. Less than ten years ago she had been an atheist. Experienced in social and sociological matters, this still young and dynamic woman had dedicated her life to the social improvement of the Basurero section of Juarez. She was also the leader of the charismatic group at Juarez. The qualities that singled her out included her intelligence, an easy manner, and a discreet yet effective presence.

She told me about the self-administered cooperative

which supports the 224 families of the Basurero. Before Christmas, 1972, the people of the Dump had, literally, been at daggers. Now they worked together. As a result they were able to throw off the yoke of chronic exploitation that had kept them in a state of squalid poverty. A poster printed in 1974 recalled one of the decisive actions: *Exploit the refuse, but not the refuse workers! (Que se explote la basura, no a quienes trabajan en el basurero!)*

A long history accounted for the rise of this association (SOCOSEMA), whose leadership is democratically elected. Among other things, the association sees to the sale of articles gleaned from the Basurero, and the payment of workers in proportion to the work they've done (this seems the most equitable and practical arrangement). It also provides instruction for those who want to learn to read and write. It engages in welfare work and makes medical help and consultation readily available.

Guillermina was present at the famous Christmas dinner of 1972. She remembered Luis, who kept cutting slices without end from two hams.

"How many slices does one ham normally make?" I asked.

"About fifty," she replied.

"Were you aware, at the time, that something extra-ordinary was happening?"

"No, it was the following Saturday, on returning to the Basurero, when we discussed it and wondered where all the meat had come from, since we were prepared for 150 people and more than 300 people showed up. We figured that we had on hand at the time 226 tamales (a concoction of minced meat and red peppers), far short of what was needed. What happened then we saw as a sign that the Lord wanted to do something extraordinary here, by way of love, and coop-eration. And so, eventually, SOCOSEMA was founded.

I began to realize more and more that among these people a miracle, if miracle there was, did not deter them from work or organization but rather served as stimulus and motivation. They look to God for help when human efforts fail or prove inadequate. And, from what they all told me, they have never been disappointed.

Guillermina, who had studied sociology, characterized the Basurero as a "subculture" and pointed out the problems encountered in promoting a better life for its people. But much progress was being made. SOCOSEMA is an instrument of cooperation in all areas. It was established in 1975, in three steps, from March 4th to May 16th, when official authorization to establish it was obtained.

"We are striving to accomplish good all around, material good obviously, but especially spiritual and cultural good in the area of human relations," explained Guillermina.

"What is the role of charismatic renewal in regard to this?" I asked.

"It instills the life and spirit of the cooperative."

Thorny Aspects of Miracle

Guillermina's husband, Dr. Antonio Villalva, provides medical service to the cooperative. I asked him about the cures I had heard of.

"As a doctor, what do you say? Have you observed these cures? Were you taken by surprise? In what way?"

"I cannot deny that there have been cures for which I have no medical explanation."

"Those who asked me to write a book about the community would like me to establish the facts relating to the cures. They would like documentation, more or less as demanded at Lourdes, by asking three questions: 1. Was there an illness, and what was it? 2. Was there full and complete cure? 3. Was it extraordinary, anything that normal medical practice could not account for?"

"We are in an area of faith, where reason is not much help," replied the doctor. "Do not try to prove too much."

This reluctance on the part of the doctor recalled the uneasiness I have so often met in this regard. I must confess that at Lourdes and elsewhere, when there is question of scientific verification, doctors tend to beg off. It is a principle of scientific medicine, as of science generally, never to capitulate to aberrant facts, never to be resigned to the inexplicable, but to form hypotheses of natural explanation until the facts stand to reason.

Though a stickler for evidence, for which one can only applaud him, Dr. Villalva was open to my questions. I brought up the cure of Tomas Salinas Lerma.

"He told me he had arthritis, diabetes, and tuberculosis all at the same time. That seems like a lot of sickness for one person."

A smile came over the doctor's face. "The tuberculosis was treated in the normal way, and the cure also was normal. The diabetes, that was more surprising. Glucose tests [for hypoglycaemia] had been positive since June–July, 1972. The control programme of the diabetes went on for five years, to the time of the cure. One day Tomas walked in and said he was cured. In 1978, it was verified. Since then, everything has been normal, and there has been no need for medication.

"The cure of the arthritis also was surprising, but the diabetes, that was the most surprising." (Later he sent me some of the medical records, which, however, fell short of what is required for authentication at Lourdes).

"The real miracle," chimed in Guillermina, "was the new spirit and determination that brought us together as a result of Christmas 1972. The whole community joined forces for the Basurero. Since then, cooperation, prayer, and conversions have all increased dramatically. Christmas 1972 was the first sign."

These last words of Guillermina reminded me of the

conclusion to the gospel account of the wedding at Cana, where water was changed to wine: "This, the first of his signs, Jesus did at Cana in Galilee . . . and his disciples believed in him" (Jn 2:11).

"For you also, it was the beginning of faith," I remarked.

"Yes, it was," replied Guillermina.

At the Bishop's

I had asked to meet the bishops of the two cities across from each other on the Rio Grande: Bishop Flores of El Paso, principal spiritual spokesman to the twenty million Hispanic Catholics in the United States; and Bishop Talamas of Juarez, spiritual shepherd of this fifth largest city in Mexico. Bishop Flores was not in El Paso during the time of my visit, but Guillermina arranged a meeting with Bishop Talamas and took us there by car, myself, Father Thomas, and Sister Linda Koontz.

The bishop's house was a modern, ground-level structure, featuring glass and opening on a flower garden of truly dazzling colors. We arrived about one o'clock in the afternoon. The heat was intense. The bishop, in casual dress, wearing a light shirt and pants, met us in the main parlour. He and I had a common remembrance: Vatican II. It is no small thing, this bond with 2,000 bishops, half of whom are still active and who more or less remember my name as expert (*peritus*) or journalist at the Council. I informed him of the proposal made to me that I write about Rick Thomas and the communities that had sprung up in El Paso and Juarez. I handed him the letter I had received from the publisher, explaining their proposal. He took his time, reading it carefully, about five or ten minutes, from beginning to end. The letter spoke of the fact that miracles, cures, and conversions had been reported in the communities at El Paso and Juarez in connection with their service to the poor. Many people wanted to know about the wonders of Juarez. A book recounting this story might inspire the charismatic movement as a whole to become more involved in caring for the poor. As a journalist, as an observer of the charismatic renewal, and as a theologian who has interested himself in miraculous cures, I would be a good author for such a book. I would need to handle the miracles carefully, documenting them according to the criteria set forth in my book *Catholic Pentecostalism*.

The bishop finished the letter and sat quietly, waiting for my question. I asked him. "What do you think of the proposal? Have you any objection, any advice to give?" He responded:

I value the zeal and personal character of Father Thomas. Hence, I would be agreeable to a serious, well-founded book. But let me offer some words of caution. Do not be tempted to see miracle where there is no miracle. Do not speak of miracle, only to discover weeks later that the person has died. [Afterwards, I learned that the bishop was referring to a specific and complicated affair that did not directly concern the community.] There should be a group of people of good judgement, like Guillermina, who can help to ensure that what was not real will not be painted as real. And take care not to put forward miracles as common, ordinary gifts of God.

These precautions I feel are necessary for two reasons in particular: so that the book will not encourage people who are ready to believe anything and so that miracles will not be seen as normal, daily occurrences. Some charismatics might like that, but other Christians will find it disturbing.

Write in a way that helps to bring Christians together. Be rigorous, and prudent. Do not relax your standards. Be careful about prophecies, which keep multiplying and are not always proved correct. As bishop, I have been made aware of pretended prophecies which claimed there would be persecution and there was none. Do not write in the manner of the old hagiography. And do not cater to credulity. The important thing is charity, the Christian love of God and neighbour, its commitment, its fruits, and the working of grace in everyday life. The important thing is conversion to charity and justice. Healing of the heart is more precious than physical healing.

Father Thomas was in full agreement with the bishop. The bishop went on to suggest that the book contain a critical introduction that would make all the necessary theological distinctions: miracle and cure, certitude and probability.

I told him that in principle I could not agree with him more, but added that in a book of this kind, which would be addressed to the public at large, a discussion of abstract principles might seem confusing and somewhat dull. Moreover, in the present climate of confusion and contradictory terminology in regard to the notion of miracle, trying to define abstract principles runs the risk of having them misunderstood and adding to the confusion.

I commented that in the press and in common parlance the word "miracle" is put to all sorts of uses. We hear of the "Italian miracle," the "Brazilian miracle," and so on, referring to technological or economic progress, which may be remarkable but is certainly not inexplicable. And so it is in other instances. Theologians, in consequence, are almost afraid to use the word any more, even in the gospel. The notion of miracles has become too abstract, so unrealistic that theological commissions appointed by bishops to pass on the cures of Lourdes have failed to recognize as "miracles" certain cures which medical authorities of the first rank had pronounced extraordinary and inexplicable. In short, it is my view that in this matter there is no geometric proof, nor even scientific proof in the strict sense. At Lourdes I have argued that we get away from this mindset which rather belatedly has been permitted to overshadow this question on one pretext or another, scientific, juridical, or theological. New ways must be found, which do justice to God's power and to the reality of his gifts, which can be striking, extraordinary, and truly astonishing. But we must not demand what he never has given: irresistible proof of that which is utterly free and gratuitous. And we must not make claims that are not made in the gospel itself.

I told the bishop that I proposed to write an objective presentation of the facts, in good faith and in documented fashion, so that everyone could judge of them in peace according to his or her own lights: the light of medical science and psychology, if applicable; the light of faith, if the reader is a believer; the light of philosophy or its special perceptions, if it has any. And if the probers of paranormal phenomena want to approach the fact from their particular angle, I see nothing wrong in that, though it seems to me that up to now their explorations of the frontiers of consciousness have not netted anything very solid. It is not impossible for God to work to the benefit of believers through the paranormal, if it exists and some day can be more sharply defined. But that would be another book, another piece of research, and beyond my competence.

My intention, I told the bishop, was to document the facts as they are, simply, honestly, soberly, reflecting the community itself, without too many distinctions or needless sophistication. I believe more in a certain "lighting up" of the truth, to *show* rather than to *demonstrate*. This is what Christ did: "Come and see" were his words. My experience in doing research, both historical and exegetical, has been that the light of faith does not interfere with the most rigorous application of the documentary method. I wanted to proceed in this open and impartial manner. I would be able to certify the facts. I did not think I could *prove* them. The marvelous in general, and at Juarez in particular, yields its truth in a certain chiaroscuro, a mixture of light and shade whose mystery cannot be forced.

The bishop seemed to agree. Guillermina summed up the meeting. Her poise and authority were evident, as was the confidence she enjoyed with the bishop, who in fact had made her the leader of the charismatic renewal groups of Juarez. Her responsibility of exercising internal *oversight* was not unlike the responsibility exercised in the early Christian communities by the *epi-scopos* (overseer, hence the word episcopate). Because of this kindred function, she was sometimes good-naturedly called, *la obispa*, as deputy of the bishop *(obispo)*.

Guillermina's standing with the bishop and in the community interested me on several counts. It recalled the advancement of women that was seen in the Middle Ages when some abbesses had jurisdiction over monasteries of men, but also because charismatic renewal often seemed to keep women in a position of subordination, notwithstanding that the women of these communities appear happy and intensely confident. Here at Juarez I sense the beginning of something different. I say this even though Mexico is not a specially feminist country, including the government, where it seemed to me the position of women was particularly second-rate. The Spirit breathes where the Spirit wills, and we should beware of trying to freeze the charismatic renewal into a rigid mould, a system. The communities that have grown up around Father Thomas drew my attention because, among other things, they are strong where some feel the renewal is weak, in social involvement and the promotion of women.

Before we left the Bishop, Father Thomas whispered a word to Guillermina.

"I need permission for the exorcism of a child."

Guillermina replied. "This is not the time."

In the car, Father Thomas asked. "About the permission, what should I do?"

"I think the Bishop would have no objection and his permission may be presumed," she said.

On our return, I talked some more with Guillermina. She told me about the activities of the cooperative, that it combines production and distribution with other services, educational, medical, and so on. Plans were afoot for the construction of 232 homes. Eight were already built. "In this community,"said Guillermina, "I have seen, in the last seven years, many cures, especially cures of degrading habits. So many men have gone back to one woman: *their* woman. All this is the fruit of the gospel: human compassion and spiritual weapons."

It was now three o'clock in the afternoon, time for Guillermina to go to lunch, and for us too. We spent the rest of the day going over Father Thomas' files. Though somewhat short on administration, and not at all file-conscious, he did have on hand an interesting assortment of letters, pictures, and documents, preserved more or less at random, with no particular purpose in mind. As a matter of fact, he was surprised to find them there, in the drawers of his suspension file, which he never has time to go back and examine. The future, the work to be done, is what commands his attention most. But some years previous he had been moved by the cure of a child by the name of Veronica Harris. He was able to obtain a copy of her medical history, which he still has on file, together with a letter containing a dismal prognosis from the head of pediatrics at Thomasson General Hospital in El Paso, dated December 27, 1973.

The child had a bone disorder called Hand–Schueller–Christian Disease. "I doubt," wrote the pediatrician, "that she will ever be well again. I am sure that she will require medication for the rest of her life."

One day at a prayer gathering, when the girl was four or five years old, she announced that she wasn't sick anymore. No change was immediately noticeable, and little credence was given her words. Yet it soon became evident that there had been a most remarkable recovery of health, so much so that Father Thomas began to assemble the medical dossier that now lay before us. However, he did not follow through on the case, nor on any other, because the work of feeding the poor demanded all his time.

Unfortunately, the community has lost track of the little girl, who by now must be fourteen years old. Her parents had moved away.

"If you want documented cures," Rick Thomas explained to me, "it is always cures of the rich. The poor do not go to a hospital. They hardly ever see a doctor. They are sick, and the sickness is obvious, and serious. Suddenly, you see them cured. You have no documents."

Yes, it is difficult to get a written history of the poor, whether in regard to miracles or holiness. I know this from my own experience, as one who has made historical studies in the church. Should we therefore ignore what evidence we have? Shouldn't we rather insist on exploring it?

The Lord's Bank

Early Tuesday morning I asked when we would be leaving, to make sure that I wouldn't be late again, like yesterday. We were to leave at six o'clock in the morning.

The house where I slept had literally been invaded by the young people who worked at the Lord's Ranch, those whom I had seen on Saturday and Sunday. Their day off from the Ranch was not Sunday but Tuesday. Today they had come to El Paso and the guest house was open to them. We were really crowded, since the place was a small family-size dwelling, which normally accommodated a half dozen people and there were twenty of us that night. The weather permitted seven or eight to sleep outside on the lawn. In the morning several of them went with me to Juarez to help in the distribution at the famous Food Bank, which operates at several locations but on Tuesdays is located in Carlotta's neighbourhood.

At OLYC this morning everyone loaded food onto the trucks for distribution. Father Thomas already had left in the first truck. We joined him at the place that served as a school and chapel. At seven, as yesterday, prayer began. There was the same pattern of spontaneity and improvisation, with dancing, praise, and prophecy. One sensed the simple joy and constant thanksgiving of the participants, who turned out in greater number than yesterday. Guitars joined in, as they pleased. Calloused hands flipped pages of Spanish Bibles. The women, for their part, prayed in another place.

About 7:30 we all went to a tent some 200 yards away, where Mass would be said. The tent, pitched in an open space among the huts of the area, consisted of a loose rigging of gunny sack flaps moored to ground stakes. A light breeze filtering through the flaps fanned the inside. But the sun was already beating down at 8 a.m., and the heat would increase as the day wore on. I checked my photographic equipment and found that I would have to make adjustments in the shutter and diaphragm, for I did not want my camera to play me false under this tent, reminiscent of Abraham's.

The altar consisted of a small, low-standing table. Near it was a stone reservoir from which people were getting water. The reservoir was a blessing for the locality, since its thickness kept the water fresh. It was a far cry from the filthy barrels still widely used by the people of the area.

In the tent, men unloaded bags of lentils and flour, fifty to sixty kilos each (110–120 lbs). A hundred bags or more were being prepared for distribution. I thought that the distribution was about to begin, but it did not come until much later, in due course, after work. No one showed any impatience. Ritual and reward unfolded tranquilly, in steps: first prayer and Mass, then work assignments, then work.

After that, the distribution of the foodstuffs would seem like the fall of ripened fruit from the tree.

Mass would begin after a time of prayer. With a competency of their own, the "apostles" and leaders launched the prayer of the assembled community, which proceeded in the usual fashion. As more and more people arrived, everything gained momentum: the guitar playing, the singing, the clapping and dancing, and the exclamations.

"Gloria a Dios!" "La sangre de Cristo tiene poder!" (The blood of Christ is powerful.)
"Viva Cristo Rey!"

Other hosannas were heard:
"Viva nuestra Señora de Guadalupe!" (Long live Our Lady of Guadalupe!)

In the gathering, children mingled with adults. Stout matrons and grandmothers carried babies. The ailing were side by side with the well. Mexicans rubbed elbows with "Americans." A friend of Father Thomas had come from Florida with his daughters: fair-complexioned young ladies who found themselves cheek to cheek with the dark-skinned children of the barrio. During Mass everybody shook hands and exchanged the kiss of peace with the same levelling of age, sex, social standing, and cultural difference.

One of the "apostles," a well-built Mexican, portly and personable, spoke directly to the sick and the afflicted, inviting them to come forward for the prayer of the community: "Come to the front. Don't be afraid."

It was not the moment for picture-taking, considering the apprehensions and inner conflicts of these unfortunates. They started to edge forward, forty or more people overcoming their hesitation at once. Those in front made way for them.

Everything went smoothly, despite the fact that people were packed into the tent elbow to elbow. All the miseries

of the community were there in the foreground, registering
in a face or an emaciated body. The prayer of the Mexican
leader strengthened and intensified. Hands stretched
heavenward. The people vocalized and prayed in a sustained
rhythm, fervent and quickening. It was not a prayer of
petition but of complete trust and thanksgiving. The Lord
for his part, it would seem, inclined to all the miseries which
they brought before him. The prayer moved in short
phrases of two or three words improvised by the leader and
repeated by the chorus of people, in litanic fashion, phrase
after phrase. The tempo accelerated, expressive not of hurry
but of growing intensity. Before the chorus had finished an
invocation the leader was already beginning another.
Succession merged into a sort of simultaneity. But the
words were clear and strong. Not a syllable was lost. And
the resonance rallied the spirits of sick and well alike.

A woman was stretched out on the floor near the improvised altar. In the dense crowd she had managed to slip to the
ground without a stir or jostle. She had found a place
between trampling feet. She appeared lifeless. I asked
myself if this was what some call the "slaying in the Spirit,"
a phenomenon that preceded some cures and conversions.
Cardinal Suenens has expressed a concern to Americans
who would make it a regular thing, as though inducible.
Here the phenomenon sometimes occurs spontaneously.
No one stops to look and wonder. Nor is anything done to
induce or bring it on. This total relaxation and
abandonment of the self can lead to surprising results upon
reviving: a sense of liberation, release from inner tensions,
or a renewed surge of hope. The head of this woman, who
lay practically at my feet, rested on the knees of her children.
People were not taking much note. They knew what was
happening to the woman. Besides, their attention was
elsewhere. Outdoors the sun was climbing, its shadows
growing shorter and sharper, in bold relief. The prayer
rolled on, still gaining momentum.

The Bread and the Body

Mass began. Father Thomas appeared in a chasuble too short for him. His voice alternated with that of the leaders and singers, who handed him the microphone whenever he needed it. Like the others, he stood on the ground and handed the microphone back to them for the singing and the invocations. It was a simple apparatus but served its purpose even though there was only one amplifier, which hung from the flaps of the tent. The Offertory took on its full meaning; here was the primitive church, people united and crowding around piles of foodstuffs destined for distribution. Week after week this food saves them from malnutrition and even from death, which in years gone by used to be so frequent, especially among children. The lay people were giving way to the priest for the exercise of his ministry.

The words, "This is my Body," by which bread becomes the Body of Christ, were the key to everything: the food, the people, the community formed into one body for a common work and the praise of God. One bread, one body, one Christ, one joy, for all to receive and share. Songs and exclamations soared from the start, ever and again but not overexcitedly. It was tranquil joy. Faces of the sick and the afflicted, who had come to the front, visibly brightened and seemed transfigured. The woman on the ground rose, quiet, placid, unnoticed. It was ten in the morning.

Work and Food

Mass was now ended. The women went off to the right, into the hot sun, and the men to the left with their tools: a shovel or pickax. They lined up outside, where the leaders assigned them their work. They split up into groups, which departed in various directions. All of them would work for four hours, according to their aptitude and the needs of the community.

Some stayed behind to stack the foodstuffs brought from a shed in the back by wheelbarrow or truck. It looked like a farmer's market. There were fresh onions, a dozen bags or so, which the women and children began to pick from; and fresh vegetables, including red, ripe tomatoes and fresh green cucumbers brought out last because of the heat. The feeble and the sick remained seated, the only ones not engaged in the general activity. An old man who was lame and practically blind sat on the ground with both hands planted on a cane between his knees.

City of Hope

Father Thomas took me to the workplaces. But before that we decided to look over the site of the future city of his dream. It was little more than half a mile away, a stretch of high ground relatively flat and sandy, a ledge overlooking the hill country. No road led to it yet, and no squatter had ventured to settle there. Water, which is vital, could not have been hauled up the steep incline.

Two days ago at the Dump I had seen faces light up when Sergio handed Father Thomas a letter from the local administration. It had to do with the expanse on which we were standing and indicated that five acres (two hectares) could be made available to Father Thomas and the community. I assumed that this welcome news was the end result of long discussions and negotiations.

"Oh no, we hadn't asked for a thing. It just came, out of the blue," Rick Thomas told me.

Surprise is a daily occurrence here, and always a message of encouragement. It supports, it blesses, and it crowns untiring effort. The impossible becomes possible. It seems to fall from heaven and is received with the kind of wonder and joy that overflows in thanksgiving. But the people do not sit on their hands, waiting for surprises to come to their rescue. They know that God helps them when they work and do their part. And they also know that the magnitude of their task always exceeds even their best efforts.

We went up to the location of the future city. It lay against a mountainous mass, not very lofty, perhaps, but still grand in the flow of its ridges, so like the Rockies. It made a perfect setting, this backdrop of nature and the view it offered.

Looking down from this elevation, one saw the real city in the distance below. Tall buildings rose from the centre, magic castles in the bluish haze. Father Thomas' city was still desert: sand and stone. It would have made a good locale for filming a life of Jesus. Its vegetation was harsh and prickly. Crouching to take pictures at the proper angle, I felt thorns stinging the flesh all over my body, right through the clothing. These aggressive spines are going to give way to human habitation.

Father Thomas explained his project. There will be homes, a medical clinic, a social centre also a church, because in Mexico, Mass is authorized only in church. The provisional Mass we had this morning cannot go on indefinitely, and the community is very eager to build the house of the Lord. Even more than the family home, it will be for each and all a common home, the foundation and inspiration of all the rest: *Gloria a Dios!*[3]

Seen from above, the barrio with its hovels of tin and cardboard took on the features of Palestine. There appeared donkeys, scraggly bush, and children. Only the sun and the children lent a modicum of brightness to the dismal panorama. This no man's land lies between open country and a glittering city that attracts rural people from far and wide in search of work. It seemed to cry out for its humanization and salvation.

Men at Work

Near the school under construction some men were putting the finishing touches on a modest home, a one-story structure fashioned of a kind of adobe brick. It had taken just eight days to build, all by hand. It reminded me of what a home in Nazareth might have been like. Three other men were digging the latrine. It needed to be deep, because drainage was a problem. A bucket was let down. Two men pulled it back up, filled with sand and gravel. They emptied it and let it down again. And so their work continued, over and over. Nearby, the red steel girders of the future school gleamed in the sun.

Farther on, at another workplace, I discovered how homes of this sort began. A dozen men working in pairs were walking back and forth. They carried a sheet, hammock-like, which bore a load of shoveled dirt: fifteen to twenty pounds for each load. With a steady hand they carried this dirt about 100 yards down the line, to a pile which other men were levelling. There it was mixed with sawdust, brought here by truck, and with water. The mixture was then pressed into wooden moulds (built together more or less like compartments of a wall shelf but lying flat on the ground, face up, so that each compartment formed a thick rectangular brick). After a while, this mould-work is turned over and the bricks fall out, still moist. They dry under the sun. Workers keep turning them, surface by surface. The sun is so strong that they "cook" in a day. They make solid building material, which protects against the heat in summer and the cold in winter; for, it snows here, in January, I was told. I would never have thought it.

Everything considered, the work in the "brickyard" was well organized. I realized there was little scope for mechanization (e.g. for an electric mixer), since there was no electricity in this area. But why transport dirt by hammock when a wheelbarrow or truck was available and much more efficient? To this question Father Thomas replied:

"Often, when we try to organize work purely on efficiency, we destroy the human factor."

"But in this case, how would a cart or truck impair the human factor?"

"In this particular case, yes, I could see no objection. But that is how the work happens to be organized."

As we were leaving, I could not but remain impressed with the way the men were doing their work, still coming and going, carrying dirt in pairs from one place to another. Among them was the teaching brother from New York whom I had met at the Ranch. I recognized him by his hat and the veil he wore to protect his tender skin from the sun, whose fury was not yet at its height at one o'clock in the afternoon. I thought of Chinese peasants lugging dirt for dams in a basket. The dams did not hold, but the effort was a step in unifying a people and assuring it cohesion and the victory they felt they had won. Rick Thomas knew how to instil comparable and even greater motiviation, a motivation founded on God. Workers, two by two, carrying dirt in a linen sheet, might it not be symbolic of the community spirit that impelled them?

More Cures

I had something to eat in a home near the place where we had Mass and where the food was distributed. There I met other men of the community. They spoke freely, coming up to me to talk and to tell of themselves.

One was Armando Enriquez Chairez, about thirty years old. "For four years," he said, "I was a drug addict." Now he is cured.

He also told me of his mother's healing. She had been subject to seizures and had suffered from a skin disease that covered her body. Hers is another cure of the poor that cannot be documented.

Rodrigo Corona Rincon, another member of the community, had been trained from childhood to be a pickpocket. He did time in prison. Now that's all behind him.

No longer is he a hunted man. His animated face, his lively hands, told of his happiness.

Miguel Angel Enriquez Chairez, who directed the singing this morning, told me how he was led to the community. For a long time he had ridiculed it. "There still are people who ridicule us, and who probably would have ridiculed us this morning, hearing us sing and pray." He went on with his story:

My family was poor. We were five children. When I was six, my father was sent to prison for selling drugs. He came out when I was eleven. He tried to make me go to school, but that was impossible because I had to work. My father was "locked up" again, for the same reason, for five years, until 1962. I drank, I sold my own blood, I stole. Often I slept in the streets. I was put in prison several times. I stopped stealing when my father came out of prison in 1968, but not completely. I was afraid he would be sent back to prison on my account.

At twenty, I got married but kept on drinking. I beat my wife. Members of my family took me to task, but I wouldn't listen. I beat my wife even when she was pregnant. I was unfaithful and took pride in her jealousy. We had three children. It was then that my wife learned of the Food Bank. I forbade her to go there. For me, they were "crazies." She went anyway. My mother went too, and backed her up. They returned with a good supply of food, which seemed to multiply at home. But I didn't care. I had never learned to pray. I did not know God and had not even made my First Communion. My wife kept going to the Food Bank, every Monday, Wednesday, and Friday. Often I beat her when she came back. Friends and my brother Armando asked me to go to the Food Bank. Then my mother asked and finally I went. When I arrived, I saw Reuben dancing for the Lord. I thought it was crazy, because I had never seen anyone dance for God. I felt like hurling a rock at him to make him stop acting like a clown. Afterwards there was Bible study, then work, to which I didn't go. But I was at the head of the line when the food was handed out.

Some time after that, my mother asked me to come to a programme of evangelization at Felipe Angeles. I didn't want to go. I had a football game. But, just to get her off my back, I agreed. When I got there, people were praying and clapping. I clapped, too, not to pray but just to make noise. Martha Medrano came up to me and said:

"Guero, Jesus loves you." She gave me a picture of Christ and left. But her words stuck in my mind and have come back to me many times. I began to sing with the others.

Conde Varela asked me, "Do you want Jesus?"

And Sister Linda said, "You are an apostle of God."

From that moment I knew I wanted Jesus. I trembled all over. Sergio and his wife prayed over me, and I had the sensation of hot water flowing over me. I slumped to the ground. I was not unconscious, but I was on the ground and felt very hot. I was drenched with perspiration. I couldn't figure out what had happened. I was very weak and couldn't get up without holding on to a post. When I came back home, it was Sunday. Some neighbour friends came with bottles of liquor and invited me to have a drink, as before. But I told them, "Not for me. I am an apostle of the Lord."

My brother, who was among them, said: "What! Apostle for what!" He thought it was very funny, and had a big laugh. "Are you sick? Want a pill or some marijuana?"

"No, honestly, I am perfectly well and feel greater joy than ever in my life."

He asked me again to have a drink, thinking that would be good for me.

Again I said, "No, because Martha wants us to be at the community very early tomorrow morning."

That Sunday was the happiest day of my life. I felt wonderful and began to sing. My voice had come back. For some years I had had a stutter and could scarcely speak, let alone sing.

It was hard to believe, after having heard his warm and stirring voice again, as I had this morning. Though still young, he had also been having trouble with his legs. But now he was the picture of health and happiness. He also told me of a surprising "multiplication of food." He knew the facts, because he was in charge of the supply store and had learned to count and keep track of stock just for that purpose. It happened in the beginning of January, 1978.

On that particular day there were 500 people at the distribution centre and only 350 cans of milk.

I thought I heard him say "canetas." "What's that?" I asked.

He wanted to show me but did not have a sample with him. He sent for one from the supply store, so I could see for myself. Meanwhile, there was a lull in the conversation, which gave me time for a bite to eat. When the sample arrived, I recognized it at once: a can of condensed milk, the sort of can in common use. He went on to explain.

So, we were 150 cans short, like this one. Not to disappoint anyone, we prepared a supplement to make up for the lack: a mixture of soy and sugar. The distribution began. Five hundred people each received a can of milk. And there was still some left. The twenty-five workers were then given two cans apiece. After that, two cans still remained. Altogether, we had distributed a total of 202 cans over the 350 we had at the start. I counted again . . . I couldn't figure it out. I spoke about it to Sister Linda. We were sure that we had made a careful count beforehand. My wife had even told me that there weren't enough to go around. And we had prepared the supplement, which was never used. It was the first miracle I saw here. Since then I have seen others. The Lord does not make a show of his miracles, but on Tuesdays we always have what we need.

I spoke next with an elderly woman. She remembered the date of her healing. "I was healed on November 6, 1978. My mouth was so twisted I couldn't eat. Even drinking was hard; I could only take a little at a time. The paralysis had gone to my throat. The community prayed and everything went away."

I gave up taking notes, overwhelmed by the sun and the miracles. I thought of the last verse of St. John's Gospel. "There are also many other things which Jesus did; were every one of them to be written, I suppose that the world itself could not contain the books that would be written."

I was also put in mind of Isaiah's prophecy, cited early on in the Synoptics: "The blind see, the lame walk, the poor have the gospel preached to them."

In the midst of all this, on Monday morning, I had intended to confirm my return flight, but the day at the Food Bank left me no spare time. On returning to El Paso on Tuesday, we telephoned for confirmation. The plane had left. But things usually get straightened out here. An hour later the problem was solved. A plane was leaving at 3:00 the next morning. At 10:00 a.m. on Wednesday I would be in Detroit, where I had been expected today. But I would still have six hours to consult with the publishers of the prospective book. Thanks to a blessed oversight I was able to take in the Food Bank and stay a while longer with the community.

Father Thomas, Sister Virginia, and Sister Linda prayed before saying good-bye, so that the Lord would inspire me. It was not yet clear in my mind just what sort of book would emerge. This incredible story—how could I attempt to tell it? And how could I appease the conflicting desires and demands of faith and the utmost prudence? Beset with so many vivid impressions, and a wealth of material that defied arrangement, I could only fall back on a profusion of prayer, which made my task seem less formidable.

Saying good-bye to the community went on into the night. A dozen young people at the ranch had finished their tour of service. They were going back to Dallas and cities to the north. Most of them did not go to bed because there was so little time . . . and so little place. At two in the morning we bundled into Bill Halloran's small red truck. He had stayed up for us. We were soon at the airport in El Paso.

After seeing these young people at work, in the sandy soil, under the burning sun, I can say that they behaved the same in the nightly environment of this modern airport: alert, obliging, congenial, sincerely and respectfully attached to each other, and even to me, the visitor. One of them was taking a different flight than the rest of us. In front of the barrier where the luggage was X-rayed, he had to tear himself away from the group. He kept looking back from the other side, but, then, decided to go through with his luggage just to prolong these last moments of togetherness.

At five in the morning I wakened from musing on the events of the recent days. We were about to land in Dallas. From there we were going our separate ways, on different flights. The young people with me led me to my flight. We embraced. Their blue jeans disappeared in a maze of *Exits*. Day was creeping over the horizon.

Thus concluded my visit along the Rio Grande, to the people, the places, the events I had wanted to know and learn about. I have set down as much as I thought feasible of what I saw and heard. What remains is to take a closer look at some of the principals in this saga of truly evangelical inspiration, the larger story as it were, plus an appraisal of the reported phenomena that brought me on the scene in the first place. To that are appended some things I have written elsewhere on the notion of cure and miracle, mostly the present state of the question—appended for their bearing on the "miracle at El Paso."

TWO

History and Background

It is important to remember that these remarkable events are occurring on the border between the United States, the richest nation in the world, and Mexico, whose development has lagged far behind the growth of its population, which today numbers more than sixty million people. The border is a study in contrast, not only demographic but ethnic, cultural, and religious.

Rick Thomas

Boyhood Roots. On May 31, 1964, Rick Thomas, then a young Jesuit, was named director of Our Lady's Youth Centre, the social centre we have visited.

What were his origins? I found him disinclined to talk much about himself, especially his boyhood, but there were indications that the tale of grace that was his life went back to those early years. At the Ranch, while we were making the rounds, I had seen him handle hunting dogs with the skill of an expert. That gave me an opening, so I said to him:

"Your family, I imagine, had a ranch with animals, and you owe much to those roots."

"That's correct," he said.

"Was it your father who taught you how to handle dogs?"

"Yes, I owe much to my father. He had great hopes for me, and I disappointed him by becoming a priest. He is a self-made man, intelligent and as good as they come. He's still living, and is past eighty. But leave my father out of it. We see each other and talk a lot about everything, except religion. Let's leave it at that, my father and my boyhood."

I abided by his wishes and will confine myself to Rick Thomas, who was born March 1, 1928, in the small town of Seffner, Florida (pop. 301), just as the Great Depression of the '30s was getting started. His father, Wayne, was from Tennessee. His mother, Dorothy Duran, was Canadian-born. The house of his birth and childhood was ringed with citrus trees, laden with lemons, oranges, and grapefruit. In 1940 he began high school with the Jesuits. He loved to fish, hunt, and ride horses. He finished high school at age seventeen and three months later, in August 1945, entered the Jesuit novitiate at Grand Coteau, Louisiana. World War II was just concluding.

From one of Rick's schoolmates at seminary I gleaned the information that Rick Thomas had been an incorrigible achiever, a fixture at the top of the class. No wonder his father had high hopes for him. He had a keen mind with a practical bent. After two years of spiritual formation in the novitiate, there was the usual pre-philosophy curriculum in college, from 1947 to 1949. Already his vocation inclined to the poor. On Sundays he chose to occupy himself with black children, members of the world's disinherited peoples. After his course in philosophy (1949–1952, in Mobile, Alabama), he taught for three years, as was customary with the Jesuits. This was followed by four years of theology (1955–1959) at Los Gatos, California, after which he was ordained to the priesthood.

A Barren Ministry. Assignment to Our Lady's Youth Centre was made to order for Rick Thomas. It permitted him to pursue his work with the poor and underprivileged. But those were the years of Vatican II and the ensuing turmoil which descended upon American Catholics with a suddenness for which they were unprepared. Many of the changes came too rapidly and led to identity crises and to the departure of many priests and religious.

Richard was not among those who permitted themselves

to be disaffected. He set to work with all the know-how and capacity at his command. He found the means to help the helpless. He succeeded in building a ministry that was efficient and well-organized, but it seemed to bear little fruit.

The Renewal. In 1969, five years after first coming to OLYC, he heard of the charismatic renewal from Harold Cohen in New Orleans, who had been in the novitiate with him. Harold was impressed by what he saw of the movement in that city and wrote to tell Rick of his discovery: "God has started something here."

Six or seven months later Rick went to New Orleans. He knew nothing about baptism in the Spirit or charismatic experiences. He had no problem with these forms of prayer, but he was not attracted to them either. He found them a little strange and somewhat disturbing.

Abie (Harold Cohen's nickname) and Rick had remained very close friends and could talk freely with each other, like brothers.

Mildly interested in the renewal, Rick asked, "When is your next prayer meeting? I think I'd like to go."

"There's one tonight. Why don't you come?"

Father Thomas delayed and arrived as the meeting was breaking up. Only Father Cohen and some nuns, Sister Mary Virginia Clark included were still there. Father Cohen was explaining some passages of scripture concerning the Holy Spirit. Rick's mind wandered. He had a splitting headache and cut short the exegesis: "I don't want to hear all that. Shoot it to me straight."

Harold prayed over him. Nothing seemed to happen. He went home and fell asleep before he was scarcely in bed.

I woke up in the middle of the night to find myself in deep prayer, an experience long lost. Prayer had come back, very simply, as at the time of fervour in the novitiate. This ability to pray has remained with me every since.

Next morning Harold Cohen drove me to the airport to see me off on my flight to El Paso. He gave me some booklets. We went through them at OLYC and decided to make our next retreat in the form of a prayer meeting as outlined in Jim Cavnar's booklet. The retreat took place in a monastery. None of us experienced the things associated with the renewal. Nothing of the sort happened. It was simply a time of solid, blessed prayer. Some weeks later, at the beginning of Lent, we had our first prayer meeting at OLYC. Again nothing in particular occurred.

As Rick was leaving he noticed a young student sitting on a bench.

The young lady had come to the prayer meeting in search of her sister. When Rick returned in ten minutes, she was speaking in unintelligible words. "What's come over her?" Rick wanted to know. He was still ignorant about this unintelligible prayer, which is called "glossolalia" or praying in tongues. The girl's prayer was real, and later it made a profound change in her life. She developed a new taste for reading the Bible and began going to Mass daily.

"You want to know what happened?" she said to Rick Thomas. "Don't they teach you that in the seminary?"

Father Rick was becoming a believer. Something had happened that was beyond him. Prayer meetings were now held with increasing frequency and fervour, sometimes at OLYC, sometimes at Camp Juan Diego, east of El Paso. Sister Virgina, who was principal of St. Anne's school in Dallas, came for a visit. Through her the group was introduced to the gift of prophecy and its effects. During prayer she spoke out spontaneously in the name of the Lord, as the Spirit moved. Her words were a light of inspiration to the group. After the end of the school year Rick got Sister

Virginia to be assigned full time at El Paso.
But there were problems with the bishops.

The Bishop of El Paso was personally opposed but said nothing. He gave us complete freedom, no doubt on the reasoning of Gamaliel before the Sanhedrin: "If this work is of men, it will fail of itself; but if it is of God, you will not be able to overthrow it" (Acts 5:38–39).

In Juarez, this form of prayer rediscovered by the new pentecostalism gave offense to the people, whose traditional piety was quite different and who were already upset by the propaganda of some sectarian groups. The Bishop of Juarez was concerned. To avoid disturbing the people unnecessarily, he forbade us to meet in his churches. We found another place, more or less by chance. It was an abandoned building, and there we met in a dingy room which was anything but conducive to praying. The bishop stipulated that two priests of the diocese be present at every meeting to monitor the proceedings for irregularities or excesses. Finding them was a problem, in this city which had only forty priests for its half million Catholics. Consequently, meetings in Juarez were difficult to arrange and attracted only a small band of dedicated people, never more than a dozen or so.

Rick Thomas kept in touch with the bishop, who was favourable in principle but cautious for pastoral reasons.

In September I went to see him, ready to accept anything he told me. I had to get out of this ambiguous situation, one way or another. So I said to him, "Tell us what you want, for or against. We will take it as coming from God. The way it is now isn't very helpful."

Not long after, on September 27, 1972, the bishop's verdict came, just before a prayer meeting that Rick had called. He did not open the letter at once, confident that it was favourable. But the bishop had taken him at his word:

Discontinue all prayer meetings until more favourable circumstances suggest a resumption.

He was stunned. As he read the letter, the first comers were arriving. What should he do? He decided to replace the meeting with a reading of the bishop's letter.

Where Does Miracle Begin? Hearing the news, an elderly woman in tears who had come on crutches begged the community to pray for her, one last time, before they dispersed. Her name was Lorenza. They prayed over her and then Rick drove off in his yellow Chevrolet, and the group dispersed.

Some days later, a boy of twelve brought him a letter written by the boy's mother: "Do you know that that old lady was healed through your prayer?"

Father Thomas went to see, and found the woman without her crutches, completely restored. Rick said to her, "Now go and tell the bishop!"

The Sunday after her cure she walked to the parish church, hale and spry. No sign of crutches. Her arrival created a sensation. The accident that crippled her had happened in 1964. For eight long years, she had always been seen walking as best she could on crutches.

Rick went back to see her. "Did you go to the bishop?"

"Yes, but he was out of town, visiting the diocese."

Rick urged her to try again. Meanwhile, prayer meetings in Juarez remained suspended, but the news of the cure spread. Sick people came and asked to be prayed for privately. One of them, Lupita Gonzalez, mother of a family, had a heart condition that prevented her from doing the housework. They prayed for her. But then, several weeks later, she was seriously injured in an automobile accident. Her husband warned that, according to her doctor's previous diagnosis, anaesthesia, in case of operation, was out of the question. The surgeon made further tests. He found that she had recovered from her heart condition. Recovery dated from the time they prayed for her, but she was not aware of it. The operation necessitated by the accident was performed without incident.

During this period of deep internal unrest, Guillermina Villalva, then still an atheist, was both converted and cured. She had been gravely ill.

Guillermina

She was born in Juarez in 1939. Though raised in a Catholic family, she was led away from her religious heritage as much by her altruistic heart as by her professional studies.

While working for an M.A. in history at the University of Michigan in Ann Arbor, and then for a doctorate in social psychology in Arizona, she made her first real discovery of the injustices around her. Marxism was making great strides among Catholics, influenced by a similar development in Europe. Guillermina herself was attracted. It seemed to her that Marxism was the social instrument of power that was required if one wanted solutions. Though she never joined the Communist Party, she began to think and work along Marxist lines.

She was not anticlerical or antireligious but felt that the church was wasting its best talent. But, for strategic reasons, she became active in the church, or rather among its amorphous masses, to organize social action groups. She worked in concert with priests who were similarly engaged (these priests later left the church, except for one, who became a bishop).

After her marriage, on April 26, 1963, to Dr. Antonio Villalva, a paediatrician, she moved back to Juarez and in the spirit of the rising liberation theology, helped to draw up manifestos condemning injustice and oppression.

But her health was declining. As a young girl she had sustained a lumbar hernia, and later a fracture of the spinal column. Over a two-year period, from 1964 to 1965, she had two children. Doctors recommended that she have no more. Irregularities of the heart made it necessary for her to unergo weekly electrocardiograms.

At the same time, the leftist groups in which she had become the motivating force began to concern her. Neither their activities nor their ideas seemed to take root. The groups disbanded. But Guillermina had qualms about giving up her role in the struggle for social improvement, a struggle that had become the goal of her life. In a quandary, she finally told herself: "Maybe the best way to get out of it is to get pregnant again, even if it kills me."

By the fourth month of her pregnancy she was spending most of her time in bed. During that time a friend came to talk to her, to tell her what was going on in the renewal.

"Do you know what the Holy Spirit is doing?"

"I don't know and don't care."

As Guillermina saw it, the charismatic renewal was a psychological or sociological manifestation. "In this scientific age," she reasoned, "the idea of an Almighty Father is outmoded, that of an Incarnate Christ seems mythical. Why not a Holy Spirit, a more abstract figure?"

Her friend persisted, and one day, at the beginning of 1972, brought Rick Thomas, who asked Guillermina point-blank:

"Do you believe that the Lord can heal you?"

"If he can do anything, I suppose he could heal me."

"Do you believe that the Lord can heal you?" Rick repeated, firm and unruffled.

"If he can, why would he bother himself with my little

problems when there are so many big ones, the Vietnam War, Biafra, and all the injustices in the world?"

"Do you believe God can heal you?" Rick asked a third time, without arguing.

"Maybe I could think it in my head, but not in my heart."

"We will pray for your faith."

They prayed, Rick and another person, who was participating for the first time in a prayer for someone sick.

"While he prayed for me, I felt a tremendous burden, a heaviness that seemed to jam my head into my spinal column," Guillermina said. She wondered, "If I get well, will I take charge again of my study groups?" The idea did not appeal to her. *She did not pray for healing,* but had a feeling it was coming anyway. She only asked the Lord to show her his will, in some other direction.

Holy Thursday was near. Guillermina had decided that she wanted to receive Communion again, something she had not done in a long time. She phoned a priest-friend, Father Juan Manuel Villasenor of Juarez, and asked if he would hear her confession. It had been eight years since her last one, the day before her marriage early in 1963, when she was twenty-three. She received Holy Communion, and at that moment the conviction returned: "It is really Jesus."

In order to rebuild her faith, she began to read. Both her husband and her mother regularly attended the prayer groups of OLYC in El Paso, and they told her of the first cures and conversions. But she still had questons. Could it be mere pietism? Or escapism? Or a form of alienation? And was it in harmony with Catholic teaching? The priests she consulted were sceptical. "The gift of tongues, cures, that was for the foundation of the church, in the first century. It's a thing of the past. This restoration today comes from hysteria."

Guillermina felt neglected when her husband went to prayer gatherings or withdrew for devotions when he came home from his medical practice. She felt frustrated that she did not share his conversion. "Why not pray when I am praying," Tonio would say.

On one occasion I was trying to meditate according to the method of St. Ignatius when all of a sudden I saw a great light coming over Tonio, who was in the next room. I saw him, arms outstretched, with a young child, and suddenly Tonio came out of the room grinning like a Cheshire cat. There was a radiance about him as he said, "Do you know that God is Spirit?"

"Really! I am beginning to understand that he is Spirit yet as real as this table," I replied.

Guillermina was now in the sixth month of her pregnancy, still sick in bed. She sent for Rick and asked to be baptized in the Spirit.

"Do you believe in him?"

"Yes, I believe."

She had faith again, or at least a deep conviction and a desire to go on, wherever God would lead. One day at prayer she felt the same weight pressing on her body that she had experienced before. This time she surrendered completely. The weight lifted. She had uttered an absolute yes, a total commitment. "*No quiero ser yo, sino tu que vives en mi.*" "I do not want to be myself, but you who live in me."

She did not realize that these words welling up from her heart, had been said by St. Paul. "It's no longer I who live, but Christ lives in me" (Gal 2:20).

I do not know if she ever made the connection. What is known, not least by her, is that it took several years before this desire was translated into reality.

Nevertheless, her yes bore fruit from the start. It made her see more clearly what to do with her life. It brought back understanding and appreciation of the sacraments and Catholic doctrine, which had long vanished from her mind but now were fashioning her life. It enabled her to pray spontaneously, charismatically, her hands aloft in praise spilling over in the prayer of tongues. The blessings she reaped were not for herself alone, however. Her conversion represented a gain for the charismatic renewal as a whole, in her diocese and at OLYC. All this was simply the grace of God at work.

But her doctors' misgivings concerning her pregnancy were being borne out. The back pains became intolerable. And her heart was giving out. She was put on sedation, and, later, a Caesarian was performed and she gave birth to a baby boy. She prayed that the baby would be all right and that God would watch over him. He did. That was June 26, 1972.

Grave infection set in from the Caesarian and the hemorrhages, which got worse in August. She was unable to sleep. Her doctors consulted together: Dr. August Dominguez, who had performed the Caesarian; Dr. Calderon Hernandez, urologist; Dr. Rodolfo Vera; Dr. Diaz de Leon, cardiologist, together with Tonio her husband; and Dr. Luis Valdés, her father. Nothing seemed to help. Her body was sensitive in the extreme. Just to touch her, or even her bed, set off frightful spasms. More doctors were brought in, notably Dr. Branch Craige, who had been treating Guillermina. There was speculation that her bladder might have been cut during the Caesarian.

At this juncture, a priest by the name of Father Hessler happened to be in Juarez. He phoned to ask if he could see Guillermina. It's important, he said. Her mother, who was keeping visitors away, was hesitant but said yes, he could come. He came about four o'clock. Ignoring her condition, it seemed, he pressed straight to the point:

> You must go and see the bishop, and ask him to authorize the resumption of prayer meetings in Juarez. What the Lord is doing is very important, and you must go at the earliest possible moment.

Before leaving, he held his hands over her and prayed.

"That day," said Guillermina, "was the first time I prayed to get well."

The next morning, at six, she felt well. She had slept all night, for the first time in months. The wound was dry, and the basin for hemorrhaging was no longer needed. The healing was spontaneous, sudden. She could walk without difficulty.

Tonio, her husband–doctor, was astonished. So was her father, Dr. Luis Valdés, who wrote: "What surprised me was the rapidity of change in a condition that normally resists treatment. In cases like this, progress is slow and relapses at varying intervals the rule."

Guillermina went with her husband to see the bishop, ten days after her recovery. "Tonio gave an account of the prayer meetings in El Paso," she recalled, "to which he had been going for seven months. I told the bishop that I had never been to these meetings. In the past, I had never asked him for anything. Now I was asking to go to prayer meetings in El Paso."

"Go and see what goes on, and come and tell me," he replied.

Some time later, in November, the bishop permitted prayer meetings in Juarez. They were held in the basement of Tonio's office, as the church was still off limits.

December of that same year, 1972, marked the preparations for the famous Christmas dinner with the rubbish pickers at the Dump. It was the beginning of close contact with the poor. Guillermina herself welcomed the guests on December 25th, at eleven o'clock. At the suggestion of Rick Thomas she climbed onto a table and viewed the crowd. "People did not yet know if we were Catholics," she remembered. To assure them she asked that everyone sing the popular hymn "O Maria, Madre mia."

Then she spoke of the joy and the importance of being together, a significant message for this group, who until then had been at each other's throats, sometimes literally.

The Dump: A Self-Administered Cooperative

Two weeks later Guillermina arranged a meeting to see what could be done about the Dump.

"I try to be the sociologist in everything. I asked those present *what they wanted.*"

They said, "A church, a school, and baseball."

This has all been provided, with the help of the bishop. In addition, a food store has been set up and water made available. The school was ready by the third Christmas, but the roof was missing. Francisco Villareal, a successful businessman, visited the Dump and had the roof put on. But much remained to be done, as Guillermina explained.

These things helped, but the social conditions remained what they had been, oppressed and oppressing. The men at the Dump were still victims of tremendous economic servitude. The poverty we found when we first went there remained.

In June, 1975, I met Francisco Villareal at the Dump. I had just returned from a conference of Latin-American Catholics in Puerto Rico. We all prayed, and it was decided to go ahead with the co-op programme we had been considering.

Earlier in the year, on March 23rd, the federal government of Mexico had given its verbal permission. The permission was formalized April 6, 1975.

I proceeded to set up the cooperative programme as a way of sharing goods according to the practice of the early Christians, as described in the Acts of the Apostles (2:41-45). "We would hold all things in common," with orderly and equitable distribution. The cooperative represented the nearest approach to this biblical model.

SOCOSEMA is the cooperative: The Cooperative

Association of Materials Handlers. All workers at the Dump are members and form what is called the general assembly. There is an executive branch elected by the workers. There are departments also, one for health and welfare, one for education, and one for labour problems.

The executive branch consists of a president, a secretary and a treasurer. Together they make all important decisions concerning sales, pricing, and expenses. Various needs are met by the sale of salvaged tin, metal, aluminium, glass, plasticware, old bones, and recycled paper cartons.

The training and education of the workers in the Cooperative was begun and continues with the help of the St. John the Baptist Community in Juarez. It is a full-time community of service. Its members devote all their time to serving the 300 cooperative rubbish pickers of Juarez and their families.

The Seed Grown to a Tree

By organizing, the Dump was able to meet the needs of its own people. But in the outlying area, the immense wasteland that lacked both water and sanitaion, deprivation continued to take its toll. Infants died or, if they lived, faced a dismal future. Undernourishment retarded mental development. At the Dump, almost everyone had had tuberculosis; it disappeared when balanced nutrition and good hygiene were introduced.

In the midst of this misery, Father Thomas moved to bring hope and relief. Through his efforts, which, he is the first to point out, were more the work of grace than his own, projects sprang up as needs dictated and as resources, human and otherwise, could be found.

The Lord's Ranch. The search for a vacation camp led to the area around Fillmore Pass (six miles east of Vado, in the

New Mexican desert) and to the water that transformed it into a fertile region. At first it seemed that it would be an impossible task to acquire this land. There were three owners, the first of whom wanted a half million dollars for his land. There was no way of getting together such a sum. The second refused to sell. The third could not be found.

One Sunday evening in the beginning of September, 1974, just as the sun was setting, Father Thomas and three other members of the community knelt down to pray and claimed this land for Jesus Christ. Four months later OLYC acquired the first eighty acres. At last, on February 9, 1975, development of the tract began.

Here's what happened. The first lot of eighty acres was bought from a woman who had refused to sell to other buyers but agreed to sell to Father Thomas when she learned that the land was to be used for young people.

A second lot of eighty acres was acquired in July, 1975. The first owner had tried to buy it but failed because the owner of this parcel of land was dead and had left no known heirs. Rick Thomas found the heirs, who later agreed to the sale.

In January, 1976, the federal government through its Bureau of Land Management made 320 acres available for leasing with an option to buy.

All these purchases, totaling 480 acres, took little more than a year. No one had looked for so much so soon, and the community was grateful.

Volunteers abound at the Ranch, more especially on weekends. They divide their time between praying and working on the land. The amount of land under cultivation grows each year, and its harvest goes entirely to the poor. For Rick Thomas, the Ranch, with its fruit trees and the land yet to be cultivated, is like a return to his boyhood.

The Lord's Food Bank. The Bank was started some weeks after the Ranch, as a result of an offer too good to refuse. A farmer, whose onion crop did not meet commercial standards, told Rick he could have as many as he wanted, provided he came and picked them. Young people got together and picked literally tons, so that most had to be stored. And so began the food ministry that is known as the Lord's Food Bank. It has never ceased growing. From OLYC it has branched out to other locations among the poor. OLYC couldn't handle it all.

The distribution on Tuesday, July 10, 1979, described earlier, was only an example of the weekly distribution made fifty-two times a year at three different locations each time. Several tons are given out every week at an approximate value of $4,400.

"The Bank is based on two biblical ideas," Father Thomas told me. "First, it is based on this text of St. Paul: 'If any one who will not work, let him not eat.' (2 Thess 3:10), and, second, it is based on the biblical teaching to provide a store of food for the orphan and widow."

"I don't recall the passage in the Bible to which you are referring," I said.

Rick Thomas opened his Bible to the Book of Deuteronomy.

At the end of every three years you shall bring forth all the tithe of your produce in the same year, and lay it up within your towns; and the Levite, because he has no position or inheritance with you, and the sojourner, the fatherless, and the widow, who are within your towns, shall come and eat and be filled. (14:28–29; cf. 26:12–13)

The food is donated, bought, or produced on the Lord's Ranch by volunteer workers. Poor people who have no other employment or resources receive a credit of $2.20 for each hour worked, which may be applied to food and groceries of their choice. They are also supplied with clothing.

At present there are three places of distribution in Juarez, (OLYC in El Paso being the parent body). They are the Church of St. Martin, Colonia Felipe Angeles, and Colonia 16 septiembre. This last is the principal distribution centre in Juarez.

Most of the work connected with the Food Bank is done at OLYC, where Father Thomas lives. Manuel Basurto and Carmen Alarcon direct the operation. He left a good-paying job as a car mechanic and she left her job as a teacher in order to engage in this ministry to the poor. "We love our work," they say, "and wouldn't change for anything."

Helpers at the Food Bank work hard. Needs always seem to outstrip supplies. Somehow, though, both ends meet. The thought expressed on all sides was that when shortages threaten, supplies stretch. One of the people at the Food Bank had experienced precisely this (I heard of at least a dozen such occurrences). He said, "But, that happens more when we have worked harder toward equitable distribution."

God is not a magician. Nor does he do man's work for him but only adds the finishing touch to his effort. This was obvious in the community.

Evangelization. August, 1977 marked an important date: the beginning of planned evangelization. As Rick Thomas describes it:

At that time the community was alive and active, but we didn't know how to evangelize the poor sections of Juarez. That month, permission was granted by the bishop, allowing us to gather in St. Martin's Church in Juarez. An announcement was made to the thirty-five members of OLYC, who prepared themselves by prayer for a ministry of preaching and healing. The meeting attracted a good number of women, who came without really knowing why. We prayed, we sang, we praised the

Lord. On the third day we moved to the Church of the Blood of Christ (*Sangre de Cristo*), only to find the doors locked because our prayer, sometimes expressed in dance, shocked some people. While we huddled there at the entrance, someone had this prophetic inspiration: "Take care of the men" (*Cuide a los hombres*).

In Mexico, men seldom go to church. On the average, there may be one man for fifty women. During the first three days of evangelization, they had stayed away. But now, outside of the church, which was providentially barred fourteen men were present. Among them was one of the future pillars of the community. Evangelization lasted the whole day, and the church was finally unlocked in the evening. Among the men was a murderer, whose life was changed: "*Yo creo en Dios, quiero servir a Dios.* I believe in God, I want to serve God."

The mother of this church-dodger, the murderer, slipped away when she saw her son praying like that. She did not return. All the men went to confession. All spoke in tongues, and all received baptism in the Spirit: a new fervour in their heart.

Twelve decided to give themselves completely to God and the community. They have become known as the "twelve apostles," a reference to the grace of the apostolate they received. Later, one of them, who was considered the head of the group, Julio Castillo, became worried about the fact that he could not read. His vision was too poor for him to learn. Would he ever be able to read the Bible? A year later his problem was solved. He had visited an eye doctor who had fitted him with glasses. What a joy to begin to learn to read the Bible!

Growth and Development. Efforts toward community improvement began to mount. It was less a question of careful planning than of seizing upon opportunity or urgent need, with recourse to prayer for guidance and motivation. Among other things a programme of continuing education and training in a variety of areas developed: reading and arithmetic, health and hygiene. There was also the training the people received in the course of working in the community. But, most important, people were taught to read the Bible regularly and to pray faithfully. That, together with energetic effort and flexible organization, characterized the whole movement.

The hub of activity was and is Our Lady's Youth Centre, Rick Thomas's command post. The Centre's principal functions are to provide social services, assist in job placement, and to minister to young and old in trouble. It is close to the American border and the bridge that crosses over it.

The first venture to be established away from the Centre was the Dump. A self-governed cooperative, it is now able to maintain itself. It has come a long way. Many a prestigious firm might envy the building that the Mexican government has leased to it. The design is rich in dignity and practicality, featuring a large room for meetings.

The programme for helping the poor, who are legion, began in August, 1975, through the offer of the onions that, were not profitable for the commercial market. More were gathered in than could be distributed. The surplus became the start of the Food Bank for the poor. In very short order more vegetables, both of the fresh and dried variety, added to the Bank's repertoire. Flour, too, and other staple food items were stocked.

The strength of the Bank lay not only in donations of money and food products but in a volunteer work force that could be summoned by word of mouth whenever necessary.

The Bank continued to swell. In July, 1978, there was another largesse of onions. In October, there was one of cucumbers. This time it was a farmer who offered as many as the people wanted to pick in two days. When he saw how grateful and well-behaved the young volunteers were, he let them pick for several more days. As a result, tons of cucumbers were added to the Food Bank. The whole thing was snowballing. At the beginning of winter, the Food Bank found itself with 6,000 donated boots, which came in handy at that time of year when even in El Paso-Juarez shoes are a necessity. The biggest problem was how to pair 6,000 unmatched boots. Generous donations of time, money, and effort, and of products and produce have always helped meet the needs.

Water. The drought during June of 1978 had created a serious water problem. Water trucks could not be depended on to make delivery. Children and grownups died of dehydration. The metal barrels that held fifty-five gallons were still there outside the homes, and twenty pesos would get them filled, provided the trucks came along. They hardly ever did.

To alleviate the crisis, the Flood Bank began as rapidly as possible to construct large cisterns at key points. The system may not have been ideal from a health standpoint, but it was certainly preferable to the metal barrels, which heated in the sun and provided a constant source of pollution. Mexican soldiers and some private contractors were hired to fill the cisterns in order to stop the rush of people dying of thirst. Rick Thomas also contacted James Smith, a hydrologist for the U.S. Water and Boundary Commission, to discuss the possibility of drilling some wells. It would be a doubtful venture. No successful well had ever been dug in the region. But it worked! A well was dug and is now pumping water.

The Ranch, which was started a little before the Food

Bank, helps to maintain it. I asked how long it would be before this property of nearly a square mile (about 480 acres) would be tamed and under cultivation? Nobody could give me a good answer. It depends on Providence and people of good will, young and old. At the present rate, it could be a matter of a dozen years or so.

The Source. At the source of everything accomplished by the communities in El Paso and Juarez is prayer and the Holy Spirit. The Holy Spirit imparts soul and vitality to the communities formed here. It is the Spirit that inspires and sustains the movement, for movement it is. There are some solid buildings, and there is serious thinking about the future. Books are kept, receipts and disbursements are recorded. It is not a disorganized venture. But the work is best described as open and flexible. It relies less on formal administration than on the Spirit's moving and on the cooperation he inspires among these men and women of all ages, social spheres, and cultures. The Holy Spirit is the invisible factor that creates a common interest, a communion among them, though they hail from such varied economic, social, and ethnic backgrounds. He gives them confidence that the impossible can be accomplished, and he alerts them to opportunities for succeeding.

Here, staff and regulations are secondary. The essential thing is the life lived and the experience gleaned from it. The gospel is a rational challenge to the rationalism of the wise and learned.

Evaluating such a movement is difficult. A rationalist would be strongly tempted to reduce the unusual to his scheme of the universe, offering explanations based on his system. Yet the realities of "El Paso-Juarez" are not truly served by such reduction.

We prefer the facts to their systemization, and shall try to let them speak for themselves, whether or not they conform to preconceived explanations.

THREE

Evaluation

First of all, I was struck by the kaleidoscopic character of life as I saw it in El Paso and Juarez. It included an extreme diversity of place and people and an unusual association of activities: work, dance, worship, and speaking in tongues. One led into the other. Depending on circumstances or need, there was also technology, as evident in the deep wells that had been drilled to provide irrigation and to help in the management of the land. But there wasn't much science in the adobe bricks, fabricated by hand from scratch, costing only the effort that went into them.

I found myself planted between two worlds and two languages, faced with facts both unusual and convincing. I was particularly impressed by the authenticity that greeted me at every turn. The people, their life, their work, and their extraordinary experiences rang true. I shall try to make a critical evaluation of it all by putting each thing in its place. As a theologian concerned for the truth, I must do no less.

Objections and Limitations

The enterprise in which Rick Thomas and his people are engaged has its problems and limitations. Some of the latter are self-imposed. A critical appraisal must deal with them.

The Food Bank. Considering the enormity of the task, what good is a Food Bank? Is it not obvious that its contribution is ridiculously small compared with the immensity of the needs that call for action right in Juarez, let alone in Mexico or the whole of Latin America, and indeed in all the world?

Other criticisms of this Christian community have been made. Poverty and privation sometimes result from oppression, and one of the ideas prevalent among Christians in the '70s was that aid to the poor is a cheap palliative or opiate and that the only worthwhile action is political and revolutionary in character. It alone can liberate the poor from injustice.

The action of Rick Thomas and his community is social. It is not political. It is deliberately apolitical. This choice, which, some would decry, is justified on several counts.

First, one could perhaps criticize it where oppression is extreme, as in some Central American countries. The government of Mexico has its faults, its single party and its inveterate atheism. It is a government that is relatively incapable of securing the general welfare of its masses of poor. Nevertheless, it constitutes to be one of the more acceptable regimes in Latin America, open to every practical improvement.

Second, leading the poor into political action could be leading them to certain defeat. Like an army commander ordering troops into hopeless combat simply to reap some "glory," the visionary mentality of certain Christians of good faith has often cost the poor dearly, when they were led into ill-considered ventures.

Third, as a foreigner Rick Thomas is in the worst possible position to lead a political movement in a neighbouring country, all the more because he is an American, a Yankee. He prefers going the way of loyal cooperation with a government which, despite its shortcomings, is committed to the common good. Support from the government has already helped to change some deplorable conditions and to save many lives.

Finally, and most importantly, the revolution of the gospel of Christ was not a violent revolution, despite doctrinaire assertions to the contrary. Christ refused to be made into a political leader for the liberation of his people, though he loved them (Jn 6:15). The apostle Paul demonstrated utmost loyalty to the Roman Empire, a persecutor, as was the Mexican government during the revolution between the two World Wars because of its philosophic suppositions, which still persist. But this has not prevented it from making concessions, the extent of which may be measured by the fact that Pope John Paul II visited the country.

The important thing in El Paso is the accent on grace, a principle which is unpredictable and which cannot be surprised. Pascal (*Thoughts* 7, 434) and Paul VI said that "Man infinitely surpasses man." God's grace infinitely exceeds every expectation. Sometimes its free gift is the only remedy in the face of the impossible. In El Paso this has certainly been the case. One may question the nature of the things that have been experienced there, but there is no question that they have been experienced: the cures and the growth and transformation of the community, both spiritual and material.

Rick Thomas' way is not political. But it is not without political import, even as there always is political fallout when the gospel is truly lived and acted upon. It happened in Poland under Wyszynski and Wojtyla (before the latter became Pope John Paul II). Rick spoke on the subject in a penetrating article in the August 1973 edition of *New Covenant*, where he preached a politics of conversion.

One of the major sins of our times is greed. Our whole lives are shot through with greed and built on the desire to acquire and possess more than we need. Our church is guilty of this sin; our society is guilty of this sin; our political system is guilty of this sin. We humans rape nature—the water, the air, the land, everything—seeking a profit, as if the water, the wildlife, the countryside, the beauty, were ours to exploit. The U.S. spends billions of dollars on defense to protect our way of life, our freedom. We talk about other, noble freedoms; but the freedom that many of us desire on the gut level is the freedom to possess and to be greedy, I have often wanted to preach God's word about greed, but I usually lack the courage: it would be too contrary to what people want to hear. Jesus' word in Luke's Gospel is *"None of you can be my disciple unless he gives up all his possessions."* The idea that material possessions can give any kind of security has no support whatsoever from scripture. In fact, scripture teaches that we need to break with our possessions to find our true security in God.

The Good News Preached to the Poor. Etymologically, the gospel (Greek: *eu-angelion*) is the good news, the glad tidings brought to the poor. At El Paso and Juarez it has indeed resurged as the good news. Human contrivances and human means are not eschewed, but they are employed under the inspiration of the gospel and for its implementation. The gospel, in fact, is supposed to have an impact on the world; it is not supposed to operate simply on a spiritual plane detached from the world. It is based on the incarnation (the humanization) of the invisible God, and takes seriously the laws of things human: the body and all earthly realities, material, biological, and psychological.

Our Judges. From the beginning, the gospel has controlled the distinct vocation of Rick Thomas. St. Paul's words could be attributed to him: "Woe is me, if I do not bring the Good News to the poor."

The good news means, for a start, that what the gospel stresses as most urgent is being done: feeding the hungry. For, if they die, how can the good news be preached to them? The numerous activities that have been initiated by the community at El Paso are motivated by the fundamental passage of the gospel in which Christ enunciated the criterion of Judgment Day: *I was hungry and you gave me no food* (Mt 25:42).

Before the distribution on Tuesday, July 10, Rick Thomas pointed to the people with whom we had just prayed and said: "These are our judges. The poor are our judges."

Christ's words in Matthew, cited above, inspired these words of Rick Thomas, which are not literally in the gospel but flow from it. Christ identified himself with the poor, as if to say that the poor are him and he is the Judge on the Last Day: "Come, O blessed of my Father, for I was hungry and you gave me food. . . . Depart from me into the eternal fire, for you gave me no food. I was thirsty and you gave me no drink."

This is what made St. Vincent de Paul say, "The poor are our masters." The Daughters of Charity who have come to Juarez to stay and work were attracted because they found there the source and very purpose of their vocation.

Evangelization or Development? Rick Thomas did not wait on idle discussion about which should come first, evangelization or development. He saw problems of distress and tackled them, the most urgent ones first. But in going to the Dump he made a discovery. He had hardly arrived when he saw that the people would not sit down together. So he first had to help them settle their differences and work in harmony. Bringing them happiness, he found, was not possible without evangelizing them. The question, however, is not how to choose between evangelization and development but how to combine them. Primarily, this is not a matter of detailed planning but a matter of following the suggestions of the Spirit, to be discerned in the events of each day.

Committed as he is to the poor and their material needs, Rick Thomas is just as insistent about the necessity of prayer and evangelization, a lesson he learned from experience. When he tried to serve the poor by human means or methods alone, his ministry was ineffective, bearing little fruit, despite his obvious intelligence and genuine Christian love.

In his experience, social service (feeding the poor, and improving their lot) is not made better by sacrificing evangelization, and evangelization does not result in the neglect of material concerns. On the contrary, it releases energies and resources for it. This is why "evangelization-or-development" is not a dilemma for Rick Thomas. It is in fact a false dichotomy, based on superficial understanding that impresses no one who has seen how the problem, if it is that, is resolved at El Paso.

In Santo Domingo, in the Dominican Republic, a priest by the name of Father Tardif had the same experience. For a long time he followed the adage that people needed social improvement more than prayer. Incapacitated by illness, he made a dramatic recovery that belied the medical prognosis. A charismatic group in Canada had prayed for him. He returned to Santo Domingo with a renewed inspiration which combined spiritual healing with social concern (an inspiration not unlike Rick Thomas'). He describes the change:

> Today it is much better. Before, drunkenness was a problem with many whom I brought into this work. But now that I am working with evangelized people, they no longer make off with the cash box or try to take advantage of others in the organization. They work together more and more effectively for the benefit of all.

If there is anteriority in this matter, it is the gospel and its inspiration. The first time Rick Thomas and his prayer group decided to visit the poorest people they knew (the people at the Dump), they had no firsthand experience of their misery and like everyone else, had more or less ignored it. They slept peacefully at night, like their fellow citizens, while around them, only a mile away, children and adults without number were dying. It was the challenge of the gospel that stirred them to action and proved the catalyst for the gift of the Spirit. *Do not invite your friends, but the poor, who cannot repay you.*

Inner Coherence. It began very modestly, with some food for a Christmas dinner in a small venture of the gospel. No one then envisioned anything further. But God, who inspired this initial step, saw a great deal more. It should be noted that for the venture to succeed there had first to be a work of reconciliation. Dinner at the Dump was impeded so long as the two warring factions persisted in their hostility. Reconciliation brought healing. It healed human relations. It made all the rest possible: return to God and common action for providing food and improving human life.

Like Christ, who came to share himself with man, it was in sharing a meal that Father Thomas and his prayer group got to know their poorest neighbours at the Dump and the impossible conditions under which these unfortunates had to work. Not only did the rubbish pickers have to pay an enormous tax, but they were denied the right to sell their pickings as they wished. These injustices reduced them to a state of subsistence that consisted of neither life nor death. But still the people kept to their job. What alternative did they have? Emigration, theoretically prohibited, was fraught with danger for the millions who tried it, driven by the spectre of poverty at home. The cooperative sprang up when the conscience of the community was aroused. It proved a blessing, achieved without violence but with plenty of slogans that expressed the workers' grievances: *Exploit the garbage, not the men!*

A Radical Dynamism. The peaceful and local nature of the change at the Dump should not blind us to its radical nature, or to the importance of its success. It was a revolution with dynamic potential.

Having become one with the poor, the parent group headed by Rick discovered the complexity of poverty, the many needs that demanded attention: food, health, and education. Where could they begin? How could they break the vicious circle of these problems?

Rick had no illusions as to the magnitude of the problems or the inadequacy of the available resources. He had to make a choice, and he explains it this way:

> We started with the problem of hunger, right here at our doorsteps. We came up with a solution that is not perfect but represents the best we can do for the present. Every week we distribute food to those in want. And we buy flour and enrich it with soybeans and vitamins. Made into tortillas, it balances the diet. Today, volunteers distribute sacks of flour at ten locations and three orphanages: 8,000 pounds every week for those suffering from hunger.

Hunger has remained a principal concern for Rick and his group, but still the weekly distribution often comes too late. Timely, adequate help for the poor can be as difficult to maintain as was delivering the mail on schedule in the early days of postal aviation.

OLYC's *Bulletin* of November 1, 1973, featured a picture of a dying infant with Rick's comment:

> This baby died of malnutrition four hours after the picture was taken. There was a hole in the head big enough to stick your thumb in. The child had not enough to eat for normal bone development. Food came too late.

The spiritual power that inspired and created projects at El Paso-Juarez and which harnessed idle or dispersed energies came from prayer, from contact with the Lord and with the enduring good news he came to bring. The Lord has need of people to bring it anew in every generaton. He exerts his influence in proportion to the instruments he finds open to his grace for the creation of new ways to meet new conditions.

This is all very simple, and all too easy to forget. The gospel, which is still the authority on this subject, tells us that the rich forget it more easily than the poor (Lk 6:24–25).

It also teaches that the good news of the kingdom is a seed of irresistible and unforeseen development. Its course is not mechanically charted. It solves problems, not by the seizure of possessions, not by manipulation or regimentation, nor by engineered efficiency. It solves problems by providing the kind of growth that is capable of making the smallest of seeds, the mustard seed, become a tree large enough for birds to come and build their nest in (Mt 13:31, 17:20; cf. Lk 13:19 and 17:6).

The bad conscience of Christians, stung by Marxist propaganda, has often led them to concentrate on the gospel's precept of material service, to the neglect of the rest. But this precept misses its mark when love of God is not in it. Conversion to materialistic poliics does not bring liberaton. It gets rid of one oppression to replace it with another. It does not make for happiness but for a life of melancholia, anxiety, and alcoholism, problems which become rampant in such a moral climate. These evils have been denounced in Poland, where a new inspiration has made them recede. That is what happened in the U.S.S.R. with the appearance of a feminist movement which seemed without object in a country which considered itself a paradise for women. This Russian movement, very different from the Western movements, did not blame "male chauvinism" but an ideological system which destroys men's masculinity and women's femininity. Tatiana Goritcheva and other leaders of this movement take Mary as their model. For them, religion is not the opium of the people (as certain Christians too easily concede) but a liberation, a source of little-known potential enabling them to reconstruct a life worth living.

These Christian discoveries converge with the microrealizations of El Paso. Progress and improvement have been the result of brotherliness and of the sharing of the gospel. Paternalism is strikingly absent. Authority is shared and functions naturally in projects and activities which are grounded in the grace of God.

Participation without Class Distinction. Father Thomas does not pretend to be a saviour. Nothing about him cultivates an aura of prestige. In a country where people sometimes kiss the hand of a priest, his hand is not kissed even though he is a benefactor. He is a priest, of course, and at Mass, when he exercises his ministry, his specific function is clear and controlling. He has his role, and the men who lead the singing and praying have theirs. Priest and leaders function by turn, and no one stands on rank. Take the matter of the lone microphone. I was struck by the way it was passed back and forth horizontally, between the lay activators and the priest, to form a continuous celebration in which the transcendent mystery of the Eucharist also assumes the character of service. And well it should, since Christ did not come to be served but to serve. At the Last Supper the washing of feet preceded the presiding at the Eucharist, on a flat table. In their daily prayer liturgy the people do not look to Father Thomas for some special word. The word of God, the prophetic utterance, these come from all and are received by all. Father Thomas' part is that of a catalyst and guarantor. He prays more than he interposes. In this way the whole community develops a capacity for self-criticism and self-edification, with all members emulating and encouraging one another.

The same is true when it comes to the handling and dispensing of goods. Everyone participates. When the food was distributed, I did not see Father Thomas giving directions. Through practice and experience the workers knew what to do. The food was neatly arranged by category and every distributor knew his place. I was similarly struck by Rick Thomas' quietness at the daily prayer gathering in the morning. Prayer unfolded spontaneously, with improvisations by the people. Coherence came from within.

Joy. Faith is not an opiate; it does not consist of passive resignation. Faith liberates, stimulates, and energizes.

This explains another and more important paradox. For these poorest of people the great gift   the joy of life—is not food. Food is necessary, and the task of providing it is taken seriously by all. But the important thing is *life* itself, sustained by food. The essential for them is to have found the Lord, to be with him, together, in fraternal community.

> Behold, I stand at the door and knock, if any one hears my voice and opens the door, I will come in to him and eat with him, and he with me. (Rev 3:20)

This invitation sums up what the people of Juarez told me, each in his own way. It epitomizes what the grace of God has wrought for them: community with Christ and community among themselves in which to govern their lives.

Juarez offers a great lesson to those who have only paid lip service to the gospel or who think of it as routine or find it burdensome. It is cause for joy to see the change that has come over these poor of Juarez, recently turned to God. Their conversion is total. They miss nothing from their past life even when that life had been more affluent and comfortable, as in the case of Concepcion. Such people now share the lot of the poor, in a continuing effort to bring them from want to sufficiency, to social development, to well-being.

The change that has occurred exemplifies the revolution sung by Mary in the Magnificat. This is not a revolution that replaces oppression by the rich with a new, triumphed oppression by the poor. It includes the rich, liberated with and among the poor in liberation from their misery.

Gratefulness pours out in their conversation as in their prayer. One can read it in the faces of the people. There is no dichotomy between those who help and those who are helped. Responsibilities vary, but everyone carries his share.

Discovering God in discovering the poor—that is the real treasure of this community. It is an experience in which I had the honour to share, an experience to make one humble.

Without Bureaucracy. This experience also invites a commitment. It is contagious and has built a bridge or passageway between the two bordering cities, with a combined population of over a million, two cities that symbolize two worlds. Yes, finding God in the poor has become contagious. It has spanned the border. It has spread beyond the communities I visited.

Because these two worlds have come together, including both rich and poor, the acquisition of food (by purchase, production, or donation) and its distribution require a minimum amount of administration and paper work. The savings are unbelievable, compared to the expense involved in maintaining the enormous and sumptuous superstructures of large international organizations; the buildings, the record keeping, the auxiliary personnel, the great sums spent on comfort and prestige. Too often, Christian enterprises try to copy them.

What has been accomplished at El Paso-Juarez, on the other hand, was made possible only through the action of the Holy Spirit, by whom the poor were evangelized. And they evangelized the rich who came into their midst. In this way the rich and the poor, coming by their different roads, met and found hope in the gospel.

This is the essential experience of El Paso.

The material fruits thereof could be detailed without end, much more than it has been possible for me to do so.

The Holiness of the Poor. The principal fruit, however, is evident in the holiness of the poor themselves.

What are the characteristics of this holiness? For one thing, such holiness lacks historical record. It is not written about; it leaves no archives but registers in the daily lives of these men and women. It is a holiness that results from receiving God's gift, simply, like a child, as the gospel requires; it is a holiness that receives God's gift as new, as never before in life. Why is it that people without bag and baggage, without a cent to their name, are more apt to take off at God's call and still keep their feet on the ground? The holiness of these poor represents a conversion, a complete turnaround of life. They have got rid of corrupt habits that breed in the filth of degrading poverty. Such evils also breed among the rich but in different ways.

My experience of captivity as a prisoner of war in Germany from 1940–1945 taught me that privation, *of itself*, does not inspire benevolent thoughts or the willingness to share but, instead, stirs self-interest and the law of the jungle. It rouses the beast in man, provokes the brutal attack, the deceits and excesses born of despair. Such is normally the case in the midst of poverty and degradation. What is more, those who have never given in to this latent savagery are not always the ones who seemed most virtuous.

People in the poor quarters of Juarez with whom I talked familiarly did not try to cover up their errant past: robberies, drugs, drunkenness, adultery, and so on. They appreciated the return to a happy family life after addiction to indiscriminate sexual adventures, to theft, violence and ephemeral gratifications that left them empty and anguished. Families that had become hell on earth have been transformed into the heaven of rediscovered love.

The good fortune of these poor still lacks some things. The house which Carlotta (and others) call her "palace" has no running water, no electricity, no cooking gas, no bath, not even an indoor toilet. But it represents an immense improvement on the shack that felt like an oven in summer and an icebox in winter and that was impossible to keep clean. It offers a setting for the strengthening of family life, in which even the worship of God stands to gain. Other advantages will come.

The good fortune of these poor is not turned inward, making each family an island. They share with one another, helping one another on a community level that keeps widening. But the transition from each for himself to each for all has not been easy. It represents a radical change, a new way of life that would have been impossible without communal prayer and the life in the Spirit, which transform the heart. It is a life of holiness, the holiness of sinners making progress. It is given day by day. No one pretends to have acquired it once for all.

The willingness to serve and toil for the benefit of all results directly from a conversion of spirit, in and through the Holy Spirit.

When I mentioned to Sister Linda that what I admired most here was the holiness of the poor, she was not surprised and went on to say:

They work better, with heart and joy, and get things done more quickly. They forgive each other. That also is new. Hatred, hard feelings are gone from here. It is simply a conversion to charity and justice. And if physical healing is common, it is because there has first been a healing of the heart, which is more important.

A few examples will illustrate the holiness of these poorest of the poor, so poor that some lack civil standing. They do not know their date of birth or the name of their family. But now, they know how to pray.

One of them, Daniel, lives in a shack without a door. The only piece of furniture he has is a bed, which he uses as a chair during the day. Born in California he knows not when, he was orphaned at an early age and eventually moved to Texas, where he was driven by poverty. He has been blind since 1976. The community brings him food every Tuesday, to relieve his desperate situation. But he cannot prepare his own food or defend it against rats. So it is hung beyond their reach in a basket. He is also defenseless against trespassers who steal it. The community has furnished him with a sleeping bag to keep him warm in winter. Daniel has a guitar, in bad repair, held together with adhesive tape. On this instrument he plays and sings to the glory of God. Sometimes when he sings, tears well up in eyes that no longer see. He can be heard singing.

> When I am sad
> I sing a song to God.
> He is my consolation.

Hilario Valdes, 70 years old, also had been blind, but on March 13, 1979, he came and announced his healing. He said:

> I do not want to be like the leper who was cured and did not return to give thanks. I come today to give thanks to Jesus for his great mercy on me. I have not been very grateful in my life, but now I want to give thanks with all my heart, and to praise God before everyone because he has healed me and given me new eyes (OLYC *Bulletin*, April 1978).

As for Maria, a woman whose story appeared in a recent report by Rick Thomas, she was received in a pitiable condition. She had long been abused by her husband, who was a professional witch. When she first arrived at the Youth Centre, she seemed more dead than alive. At the first Bible class she attended, one of the participants expressed the fear that she might fall over dead. But she got well and now wants to live. She spends her days praising God in song, but she also works with her hands, knitting sweaters. And she teaches others to crochet. "Her youth has been renewed like the eagle's," wrote Rick Thomas. She has found happiness and enough strength to help others.

These cases, picked at random from among hundreds, recalled for me an episode in the life of the martyr-deacon St. Lawrence. Summoned by his persecutors to hand over the treasure of the church, he brought with him the poor of the ecclesial community and, pointing to them, said: "Here is the treasure of the church."

Never had these words been brought home to me as they were at El Paso.

FOUR

Miracles:
Can There Be Proof?

One would like to stop here. But this book must also speak of the "miracles" of El Paso. The true miracle, and the most beautiful, concerns the spiritual and material reclamation of the poor. The healings, cures, and marvels of God all come as "extras." These are part of the story and should be accepted as such, however one chooses to interpret them. The reader who has come this far will know that it is not a question here of *proving* anything. I do not intend to indulge in idle repetition, retelling cures and healings described earlier. My purpose here is to attempt to *evaluate* these astonishing phenomena. They are astonishing in the root sense of the Latin word *miraculum*: miracle, which comes from *mirari*, to marvel, to be astonished at.

I have reported in good faith testimonies told in good faith, told in the honest, artless manner one does not find with the calculating witness. Admittedly, good faith can be mistaken. But those who question this report can always go and see for themselves. I do not think they would find anything to fault me, except such variants as are always found in independent testimonies and perhaps an occasional embroidering of enthusiasm.

If I do not propose to prove anything, it is mainly for two reasons already explained.

First, though miracles of the poor may become known in the community in which they live, generally there are no records, no documents to prove them. The best-documented cures of El Paso-Juarez are not those of the very poorest, yet even these would not satisfy the requirements that have been developed at Lourdes, requirements that, in fact, are almost never met. At Lourdes, the requirements have become so stringent that the authentication of cures has been reduced to a trickle, if that. In the eleven years from 1965 to 1976 there was not a single medical acknowledgment of a miracle. Later, two miracles were accepted one in 1976, thirteen years after the cure, and one in 1978, eight years after the cure. But unless better criteria are found for judging these gifts of God, the authentication of miracles will remain at an impasse.

Second, and more fundamentally, miracles of the gospel and Christian tradition are not well-suited for the scrutiny accorded them by the scientific method. Scientific examination can no doubt contribute something, but its effectiveness is limited. It can determine whether and to what extent there has been a cure, and whether it was astonishing or exceptional. But the scientific evaluation does not touch the spiritual effects which a cure may have had on the subject or those who witnessed the cure. This aspect seldom appears in the particulars of the evidentiary depositions.

Two centuries of methodical verification of miracles, beginning with Benedict XIV, have shown that even reasonable and necessary efforts to verify God's marvels can and most often do end in impasse, for more reasons than one. At the turn of this century those who thought that miracles should and could be authenticated dreamed of producing absolute proof by showing that a miracle was a clear exception to the laws of nature. Theirs was a utopian dream.

At the time it was thought that one solidly proven miracle would destroy *scientism*, with its pretension of being able to explain everything and with its absolute, a priori denial of miracle. But scientism has since died of itself, and science now is less doctrinaire and more modest, more humbly respectful of the unexpected as a datum of experience.

On the other hand, in the gospel it is not at all evident that the nature of miracle constituted an exception to the laws of nature. In the language of the gospel, miracle is a visible sign (*semeion* in Greek) given by the invisible God. It is also something marvelous, astonishing, stupendous (*teras*) that speaks of God by breaching the habitual, the common and customary. Nowhere does Jesus say that he intended to make an exception to the laws of nature or to contradict them. That may have happened, but compared with the Christian and religious content of miracles this peculiarity is a very secondary thing, notwithstanding the fascination it has held for many intellectuals, including theologians. It is this content that will also escape scientific verification. The controversy over what is contrary or contradictory to the laws of nature not only muddles the notion of miracle but tends to undermine its acceptance as a grace of God for the people of God.

Even when the documentation is most impressive and points to something like contradiction or exception, as with some of the miracles at Lourdes, rationalism in principle always has a way out. It always asks for something more. This is what struck me on the occasions when I took part in the certification process of miracles. There were always doctors who voted against verification, because they wanted one more test. And if they had got it, I think they would have asked for still another, without end. In so far as they stood on norms and postulates of the scientific method, the dissenters no doubt were in the right. Is it not a basic postulate that everything in nature can be explained? Hence, if something *appears* to be inexplicable, the normal scientific course is to look for an explanation for as long as necessary, whether it takes months, years, or centuries.

Miracles: Did They Cease with Christ?

Whether one speaks of the "miracles" of Juarez or prefers some other term is immaterial. Even the gospel terminology varies. More to the point, and this is what struck me, is the analogy between the way the marvelous keeps springing up today in Juarez and the way it kept springing up around Jesus and around the apostles in Acts. I am not saying that the facts of Juarez and the facts of the gospel are on the same plane. I want to make this as clear as I possibly can so as to forestall the severest critics. That they are not the same is plain enough. The reasons are many, and theologians have not failed to expound them. It is not my intention to question the reasons themselves nor the cultural diversity between ancient Palestine and modern-day Juarez. But it seems to me that the theologians have taken it upon themselves to exaggerate the differences, suggesting that unimaginable marvels occurred during the time of the gospel, which were meant to be phased out as the church grew older.

An engagement gift for the early church, said St. John Chrysostom about these charisms. But with more or less misogynist feeling, he added that it was no longer the season for them after the marriage between Christ and the church.

He said this of glossolalia, which had disappeared in his time but has since sprung up again, in many places, including El Paso-Juarez. The teaching represented by St. Chrysostom guarded the church against the dangers of illuminationism. But it also opened the door for a Christianity that was spiritless, morose, without hope, and incapable of responding to the gifts of God where God was prepared to continue them.

In the name of this same principle of transcendence (in itself a perfectly true and respectable principle), Pentecost has been represented as something that happened once, in the beginning, for our retrospective admiration; it is not seen as a source that could be communicated across the centuries. Great moments in the history of the church tell a different story, showing that where the integral evangelical life abounds, so do the marvels of God: marvels that thrive in poverty, in humility, and in the shadow of the cross, marvels which have never been eliminated from this world. Names leap to mind: Francis of Assisi, Ignatius Loyola, Teresa of Avila, Vincent de Paul, Catherine Laboure, Bernadette. Nothing in the gospel suggests that the post-

Jesus era was to be a time of *less*, but in fact of *more*:

> Truly, truly, I say to you, he who believes in me will also do the works that I do, and greater works than these will he do, because I go to the Father. Whatever you ask in my name, I will do it, that the Father may be glorified in the Son. (Jn 14:12–13)

With all due respect to the uniqueness of the gospel, it should be frankly admitted that from the view of secular history the miracles of the gospel and those that happen today appear similar. This is hardly surprising since these gifts proceed from the same God, the same Christ, the same Spirit, in human communities receptive to the same grace. And this face is more important than abstract distinctions that have become hardened through a sort of reflex defense of their validity. The methods and rules of examination cannot be different. The problems faced by the historian (who studies the miracles of the past) and the journalist (who studies the miracles of today) are exactly the same. And their methods of verification are not essentially different, either.

From the standpoint of objective verification, it is easier to examine the "miracles" or signs of today, since they are closer in time. Direct witnesses can be interrogated. Material evidence can be found in a variety of places: medical testimony, analyses, radio and television libraries. These sources facilitate verification and produce a more accurately documented case. None of these helps are available for any miracle of the gospel.

The method of authenticating miracles or identifying what about them was most extraordinary is not the important thing. What is important is the source, the quality of the love involved, since it is God's love that cures and the communication of his love that lifts human means and capabilities above themselves. For such marvels no geometric proof is possible.

The test for discerning a miracle as here understood is the test set by Jesus in the words: "Come and see."

It was in this vein that the man born blind spoke to his detractors, those who questioned his cure: "One thing I know, that though I was blind, now I see" (Jn 9:26).

Above all, one point is clear: The things that have happened in the life of the community at Juarez are astonishing. People who have been healed or cured were astonished. People who had suffered from a tragic lack of food, who had always found *less* than enough, began to find *more*, from the time of the famous Christmas dinner on. They remain stupefied and grateful but do not revel in their stupefaction. Their joy is expressed in thanksgiving. And thanksgiving has prepared the way for other astonishments, which it seemed only fair that I should share with the reader.

Rational Explanations

The facts I have presented are left to everyone's judgment. The unbelieving rationalist will adopt the only attitude possible for him: that there is a rational explanation. He will theorize, even as I have theorized, to account for facts that play havoc with ordinary experience and categorization.

Collective illusion? This is the simplest explanation. But it is not convincing, because the society of El Paso-Juarez is realistic. It is the hard world of the poor, faced each day with getting the necessities of life. The poor do not confuse *words* with *bread*. They continue to lead a trying material life. They work hard and keep good accounts, reckoning with tomorrow. Autosuggestion, idealizing, escapism, these are foreign to their way of life. They are not visionaries. They have an awareness of what is real, both in the human and the material order. They also have a sense of humour and and are not easily duped. They know the scepticism with which they are viewed by many others outside the community. Once they, too, were sceptical, before it all happened.

One could also consider unknown factors, psychological and social. Or one could argue from analogy. Both approaches are open to the believer as well as to the unbeliever, because God does not act among men as a *deus ex machina*. In becoming man, God did not alter or rend human nature but assumed it with all of its conditions. Hence, it would be perfectly acceptable to conduct psychological and sociological studies of what has happened at Juarez.

Personally, I have neither the means nor the inclination for such an undertaking. Transform this living community into a systematically controlled laboratory—how does one do this without prejudice to its very life? Halting a bird in flight to study the movement of its wings endangers the flight and invites a fall.

Dr. Mangiapan, president of the medical bureau of Lourdes, has advised more than one charismatic group to eschew the verification process for any of their experiences of the marvelous. You will lose your spontaneity. Guard your freedom.

For a number of cures a psychosomatic explanation may offer a plausible explanation, considering that in sickness the healing powers of the organism are stepped up. But why are the cures so numerous at Juarez? And what of the cures for which psychosomatic explanation seems clearly inadequate? To the believer, it means that the gift of God is there. He heals souls and bodies. The social services established by the community include the use of normal medical means. Any results beyond these means come as a plus, an "extra," supplying what human weakness cannot.

This gift of God, this love of God does not lie inert in the soul. It affects the conscious life and the whole body. Physical cures come as an overflow, a bonus. Sometimes they are extraordinary.

Multiplications of Food

Multiplications of food are more perplexing to human reason. After the first multiplication on Christmas, 1972, there were others. Here, in summary, are those for which we have obtained testimonies:

1. Multiplication of flour, Monday, December 10 or 17, 1975. Carole Raymond, an American from El Paso, was preparing a mixture of flour for making tortillas. She was surprised that the sack from which she was scooping the *maseca* (corn flour) was not diminishing in proportion to the amount she was taking out.

It began when I mixed the first ten pounds. I had about a half pound left over after filling five bags of two pounds each. I thought I had made a mistake and took great care in weighing the second batch. But again there was a large surplus. This time I was really annoyed with myself for not having caught my mistake, because the amounts must be precise to ensure dietetic balance. So I did the third batch, even more carefully. This time there was three-quarters of a pound too much. I couldn't figure it out. And then I thought of God. . . . (Written account of Carole Raymond, undated, some weeks after the occurrence.)

2. Multiplication of grapes, July 1977. The first pickings of grapes at the Lord's Ranch had been sent to the Food Bank. None of the workers had eaten any. They sent them all to the Food Bank of Juarez for their poor brothers and sisters. There were only twenty-six small boxes of grapes measuring $10\frac{1}{2} \times 6 \times 13$ inches. Each of the 400 or more persons who had come for a healing service received a generous portion. At the end, there were grapes left over. (Testimony of Rick Thomas, confirmed by the independent testimony of Martha Medrano, dated July 29, 1977.)

During prayer Rick Thomas had pointed to this first delivery of grapes, insufficient for everybody there, and thanked God in advance for what he would do. "Each person received from one to two pounds of grapes, and some received a double portion," declares the Medrano testimony.

3. Distribution of December 12, 1977, on the feast of Our Lady of Guadalupe. Avocados and tortillas were distributed to a crowd of 500 people. The expected shortage did not materialize. (Four written depositions: Isabelle E. Medrano, January 1978, Romelia Irrobali, Esther Padilla, some oral testimonies.)

4. Distribution of 350 cans of milk, one each to 500 people, with some left over, in January 1978. (Miguel Hernandez, as told to the author.)

5. Distribution of four hampers of grapes to 500 people in July 1979. (Attested by the testimonies of Carmen Alarcon, August 6, 1979; Carole Thompson, a visiting Canadian, 155 Balmoral Avenue, Toronto, Ontario M4V 1J5, same date; Joy Aiken, also of Toronto, same date; Jeff Wallis, 8158 Schaffer Drive, Dallas, Texas 75227, Eric Wallis, same address.)

6. Abnormal filling of sacks with squash while they were being picked. April 1980. (Testimony of Lorenza Ledesma.)

To finish with these testimonies is not really to have finished. In many quarters, questions will remain, denials persist. Speak of conversions or prayer, and it is all credible. Speak of cures, and it is still credible, those cures generated at the frontiers of consciousness where biological and psychological processes appear indistinguishable. The nonscientific term *psychosomatic* may serve to describe them. In the multiplication of food, on the other hand, reason is assaulted. Words fail. The intellectual is at a loss for coherent speech in the attempt to integrate attested fact with the accepted order of things.

The mind is drawn in two directions, neither of which leaves it satisfied.

The first and more common attitude consists of a priori denial. The alleged fact is said to be impossible, contradictory, hence illusory or attributable to chicanery. The denial is maintained regardless of the merit or demerit of its argument. As we have seen, this line of thinking will not suffice. It is supposed to be scientific, i.e., based on the a priori postulates usually associated with the scientific method. But it is not really scientific because all it can offer are stereotyped explanations based on some far-fetched analogies which themselves are based neither on fact nor verifiable validity. Yet *scientific*, of its very nature, means *verifiable*.

The other attitude accepts the astonishing fact or facts that baffled the witnesses, it admits that these cannot be explained and attributes them to God, especially since these facts occurred in the midst of a believing community, much as in the gospel.

To each his option: a priori reduction of the facts to preconceived principles, or acceptance of them for what they are.

The uneasiness under which this option will be exercised reflects the ambiguity of the word *miracle* itself. An historical study of the notion of miracle shows how simplistic the definition of miracle was that prevailed in late scholasticism and was reinforced in recent centuries with the development of determinism. Central to this definition is a distinction between ordinary gifts of God, which are in conformity with nature, and extraordinary (miraculous) gifts characterized as contrary to the laws of nature, or at least outside of its laws. Miracle, then, would be an exception, a perturbation of universal determinism: against or beyond nature. In this formidable definition a secondary aspect, which is rare and obscure, is made the essential or specific property of God's marvels. As a result, the theology of miracle has reached a sort of impasse. Theologians have become wary of the word, if not of the very idea, of miracle.

But, as often happens where excessive inhibition prevails, secular language has taken its revenge. At a time when clergy shy away from the word "miracle," even in regard to Lourdes, and bishops will not vouch for a "miracle," we find common speech applying the word to surprising events and developments everywhere, not least in the economic and sports world, as we have seen. The frequency of this word in the daily press, and of other words which have fallen into disuse in sacred language, contrasts with the excessive distrust of a theology that is caught in a system of half science.

To each his opinion. Asked for mine, I would be tempted to say that miracle, like Zeno's motion, is impossible, contradictory, because the thing moving would have to be in one place and another at the same time. Yet motion exists. It is its own proof. And that is how Socrates proved it, by getting up and walking, when he could find no answer for Zeno's arguments. The experience with God that the communities of Juarez have had presents a similar paradox. Which way should one turn in the face of this experience? The easy way out is to discount it: the more difficult way is to accept it. Placing it in doubt preserves one's intellectual security; admitting it though not reconciling it with reason involves a risk. Which is the better choice? Lacking scientific proofs in this domain of light and shade, so filled with humanity and a divine presence, I can only leave the choice to the reader.

The Essential Certainty

One thing is certain. What matters is not the multiplication of food. What matters is not whether and how food was actually multiplied but that those who were sick and dying from hunger were fed. What matters is that abundance followed on want, despite the disproportion between means and ends, between what was available and what was needed. What are important, more than these miracles of *having,* are those that touched *existence* itself. It is the cures, more numerous than the multiplications. It is the conversions, more numerous than the spectacular cures.

More important still is God's gift, which thrives in the holiness of the poor, and in the communion of Christian charity. And still more important is God himself, his communication and his sharing of himself.

As for the overflow of this gift, the marvels of El Paso-Juarez which defy our accustomed ways and our reason, why would God offer special proofs, when he refused them to the scribes who asked for signs from heaven? (Mt 12:19–39; Mk 8:11–12; Lk 11:16, 29–32).

The certitude that God gives those who live and share this sort of experience is not the same kind as that found in a laboratory. It cannot be weighed on a scale. It can only be weighed in the living experience itself and in the light that illuminates the experience.

FIVE

The Tree Grows

Since my visit to El Paso, the tree has never stopped growing. Like the mustard seed of the gospel (Mt 13:32), it is thriving and bearing fruit: materially, for the poor and hungry and, above all, spiritually. It is this spiritual fruit which brings the people the joy of God and makes them great evangelists.

Activities at the Lord's Ranch have expanded and diversified. An underground irrigation system has been installed, which is fed by a mile-long pipeline running from the two wells. The levelling and cultivation of the land is progressing. So is cattle raising. The Ranch has begun to make cheese, and a cheese-dairy is under construction. Dormitories have been constructed on plots that are not suitable for cultivation. The Blessed Sacrament has been installed in a permanent prayer hall.

The Lord's Food Bank Clinic (a dispensary started by Doctors William A. Roberts and Chris White, 4820 Isla Terra Nova, Juarez) is open every other Sunday during most of the year and every Sunday during the hot season, when the heat can be murderous because of the danger of dehydration. Services at the Clinic are provided by volunteers.

In July–August, 1980, a well was dug at la Mesa, the new location of the Food Bank, which is located not far from Carlotta's house. The well's water is excellent. A reservoir with a 10,000 gallon capacity has been built. Pipes connect the reservoir to the well, and water is pumped from it at the rate of nine gallons a minute. This represents a vital improvement, which recalls the prophecy of Isaiah (55:1–11), "All you who thirst, come to the waters."

On June 15, 1981, the Lord's Food Bank gained title to fourteen acres up on the hill of the Mesa. This is where the city of Father Thomas' dreams will be built. Electricity became available there on April 17. A supply store for the community has already been set up, and a dental clinic is under way. The great dream of building the community on this site is taking shape, with the cooperation of all.

Prayer groups are growing. Conversions and healings continue. Evangelization is being intensified. The third campaign, December 1980, at St. Martin de Porres in Juarez, was filmed by Bobbie Cavnar. The film retraces the history of the Lord's Ranch and the Food Bank, together with testimonies of conversions and healings. It was presented to Pope John Paul II during the Fourth International Conference of the Charismatic Renewal, in Rome (May 4, 1981, just nine days, before the attempt was made on his life).

Evangelization has made great strides among the world's most disinherited people.

Prison Ministry

Sometime in 1978, the director of the city prison of Juarez, Jesús Galindo Fernandez, came to OLYC to ask for Rick Thomas' help.

"These people are without hope; they are incorrigible," he said. "Only the power of God can change them. We'd like to have you come and help us in any way you can."

To prepare themselves for this new ministry, the community made a retreat from August 17th to 19th, 1979, at the Lord's Ranch.

"The first visit was unspeakable," writes Rick Thomas. "The stench of urine filled the place. Prisoners were yelling, jeering at us, cursing. Even with the loudspeaker we had brought our voices could not be heard in the uproar."

Confident that the Lord could do the impossible, the

After the horrible oil drums of stagnant water . . . the cistern of fresh water.

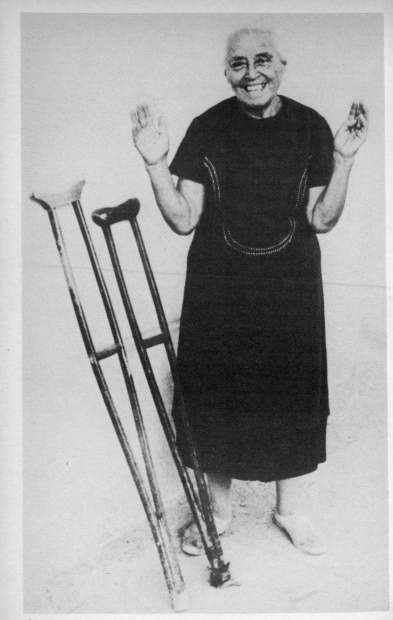

Lorenza's cure.

6

37

Miguel, the store manager, explained his perplexity to me when the abundance of food far surpassed his careful estimates.

Distribution at the Lord's Food Bank.

8

The new medical clinic. The lives of many children have been saved here.

Juarez's prison. The dialogue began here, through the sinister bars of the jail. A new prison has been constructed since the first Wednesday visits that changed everything.

Juarez prison. Food for the prisoners who await liberation and liberty.

The women's section of the new prison in Juarez. Song and dance mark the change in their lives.

Juvenile detention home. A future breaks on the horizon.

Juvenile detention home. Miguel Angel Enriquez, a former prisoner, proclaims the Good News that he himself received.

Psychiatric hospital. Contact had to begin through the protective bars, which little by little have become superfluous.

The first three houses of La Mesa, the "city" that Rick dreamed about. A new food bank began there in the fall of 1981.

The sad barrio around La Mesa.

On the left, Jésus and his friend Manuel and Manuel's grandson, standing in front of Jésus' home, a shack attached to a larger house. They work at the Food Bank.

The home of a family who comes to the Food Bank.

This woman is unable to walk to the Food Bank, so workers visit her at home to bring her food.

La Mesa. Men dig dirt from the surrounding hillside to make adobe bricks for the homes.

Two of the men on the work crew at La Mesa take time out.

Florenzo, one of the "apostles," is in charge of a work crew at La Mesa.

The pregnant women spend the work time at the Food Bank knitting for one another and their children.

After having received his food, one of the workers heads home.

The older women spend the work time in prayer for everyone else's work. Now they are ready to head home with their food bags.

Children at La Mesa sitting along the wall that surrounds the straw used in making adobe.

A married couple near their home which the Food Bank built. Power lines are evidence of the recent addition of electricity to many homes. Running water is still not generally available.

musicians that had come with us began to play a song based on Philippians 2:10–11: "Jesus is his name. Every knee shall bow, every tongue confess that Jesus Christ is Lord."

After an hour-and-a-half these words came true. A number of inmates were on their knees weeping. Several sank to the hard cement floor of the prison. The tension at the beginning had given way to total relaxation, a sort of calm and peaceful swoon. Some experienced what is sometimes referred to in charismatic circles as "resting in the Spirit."

"In this new atmosphere the guards, at first on the defensive, opened one cell to the visitors. Prisoners began to flock to us, asking us to pray over them, for them, and with them. About thirty-five thronged around us, and many felt a deep experience of the Lord."

The warden was dumbfounded and remarked that the first to come forward were the most incorrigible of the prisoners.

A second cell had to be opened, with a similar throng of prisoners.

Since then, community members visit the prison every Wednesday morning, at ten o'clock. Little by little, week by week, everything has changed. Gone is the stench of urine, and the jeerings and cursings. Even the brutalities of the guards have lessened. And no one resents the visitors.

The visiting team is made up of poor people from the Lord's Food Bank. Some of them have been in prison themselves, for theft, drug peddling, and other crimes. They witness to their own experience and to their new life in the joy and victory of Jesus Christ.

There has even been a multiplication of food in the prison, on Wednesday of Holy Week, April 15, 1981. In response to my request for more definite statements of the facts, Father Rick sent five eye-witness accounts. I will include one of them here. "On that day," Rick said, "prayer began with Proverbs 9:1–6: 'Wisdom has built her house. . . . She has set her table. She has sent out her maids to call. . . . Come, eat of my bread and drink of the wine I have mixed.' We understood that this is what Jesus does for us."

Sister Mary Virginia then told what happened.

The Lord promises great blessings to those who partake of food made with so much love. Many things will happen in the hearts of any who partake in such love of God. The food is a powerful sacramental today. The Lord wants faithful hearts in each of us. It is the faithful heart that causes his power to be released to all here. . . . So many graces are here today that the clouds of God's presence are here.

A reading of Psalm 140:12–14 and 141:5–7 inspired Sister Mary Virginia with this prophecy: "The meal is a very healing meal for all. . . . The power of the musicians is great as their hearts are humbled before the Lord. . . . Within their hearts and minds the truths of God come again and again with such beauty that they must stop and receive this special beauty from God."

After that came distribution of food in the nine cells in which the prisoners were detained: 170 in the first cell, 230 in all. We had four containers of bread pudding, each of which had enough portions for from forty to fifty people. Normally, the four containers should have been exhausted in the first cell. Yet every one of the prisoners received all the pudding he wanted, and there was enough left over for those who asked for a second helping. In addition, guards and officials received their share, and the containers were not empty until the last minute, when nobody wanted any more.

I had noticed the disproportion between the food we had and the amount that had to be served. It occurred to me that I should tell the person passing out the pudding to reduce the portions. But then I thought to myself: No, they have provided for the distribution. They can see how many people there are to feed, and God will take charge of everything. It was when I saw what had happened that I spoke. And then prayer and praise flowed from our hearts.

It was the same with the twenty-five kilos of tortillas: twenty-five tortillas per kilo, for a total of 625. We distributed them at the rate of four to a prisoner. That should more than have exhausted our supply as early as the first cell. Yet there were four to each prisoner till the end.

Same thing for the fifteen gallons of lemonade served by the women in our group. At sixteen cups per gallon, there should have been 240 servings. Not only was there enough to go around, but many prisoners were given some to take to their cells.

Armando Enriquez brought some pudding to a police officer who was interrogating a young man in his usual rough manner. After accepting the pudding, the policeman's attitude toward the prisoner changed. He was friendly and more understanding.

"Great was our joy on that day and bubbling over," concludes Sister Mary Virginia. "We laughed; we wept; we praised God. We sang to the Lord."

Today, October 28, 1981 [writes Rick Thomas], I spoke with some prisoners in a cell to which I was given free access. That was not allowed in the first week. But now, trust prevails and we have every accommodation. There were four transvestites in a small cell. One of them came up to me and said he wanted to change his life. We arranged to have him transferred to another cell, where he prayed with us. Then he renounced his transvestism, ripped off his female undergarments and kicked them away with his foot. We cut his hair. He now accepts himself as a man.

The Work with Young Delinquents

Rick also tells of a "new venture in the Lord," among young delinquents.

On February 9, 1981, the director of the *Escuela de Mejoramienco Social para Menores* (School of Social Rehabilitation for Minors) approached us with a request for our help. We accepted. It is "home" for young Mexican detainees, a stone's throw from the Rio Grande along the Mexican–Texan border.

We go every Monday morning. We begin with prayer outside, before entering the white building. Then we ring the bell and the action begins. There are about seventy boys and some girls, seven at last count. We divide them into three groups, according to the three sections in which these children are kept. We proceed as in prison, with some adaptations.

First, we get the children to sing hymns and praise God. Then we tell them that God loves them and wants to help them change their life. After that we take them individually, those who want to, and teach them to pray. They ask God to change their heart, and every week we see deep experiences with the Lord. This is the bright side of our ministry.

The other side, the sadness, is the degradation that produces these juvenile delinquents. In May we found two boys only four years old, under detention for stealing some rings. Asked why they did it, they said, "To give to the girls."

The same day we spoke with two orphaned sisters,

twelve and eight years old. They had been taken into custody by the police after running away from their aunt's home. The woman had the means but refused to pay the ten dollars for their release.

We try to follow up on prisoners and delinquents who are set free. But it is not easy. Many have no home and live in the streets or under bridges.

Rick gives this example of their work:

Juan Munoz is happy now. When we first met him in a small cell at the Hospital Civil Libertad (the mental hospital), he had nothing in the world to look forward to. Every Wednesday we prayed for him. We administered blessed salt, holy water, and holy oil. At the eighth visit he had been released, and we saw him no more. But three weeks later, visiting the prison, we found him there. He was alone in a dark cell that was smelly and cramped. Hearing the musicians of the Food Bank, he was suddenly filled with hope.

"I need help," he said. "Whenever I drink beer I go wild. I try to kill myself, or others."

"Do you want Jesus to heal you now?"

"Oh yes!"

We administered holy oil again and prayed for his complete healing. Some days later he was released. Two weeks after that, I don't know how, but there he was inside the prison, but this time he was here as a visitor along with our group. He wore a big smile on his face and played the guitar with our musicians. At one point he grabbed the microphone and told the inmates how Jesus had given him a new life. The guards were probably more flabbergasted than anyone to hear this man, a would-be killer only two weeks ago, talking like that.

Every Monday, 80% of the young detainees in the white

building yield to prayer. It is an impressive sight, these tense and exasperated children "resting in the Spirit." They lie flat on the cement floor, sometimes for an hour or longer. And when they get up, they are different, filled with hope and peace. After this inner healing their witness is infectious. Doctor R.P. Lopez, the director of the School of Social Rehabilitation, is delighted with the results and cooperates with us. The atmosphere of the "home" has changed.

The director has asked us to come every day, not every week. But where can we find the time? We haven't found it yet.

At the Psychiatric Hospital

About the same time as they began to visit the prison (la Preventiva), the community began to visit the Hospital Civil Libertad, the psychiatric asylum in Juarez. After much hesitation, the administrator of the hospital allowed community members access to the patients. In the words of Rick Thomas, this is what they encountered:

> We found there, behind bars, what might have been a lunatic man or woman. We prayed and administered salt, water, and oil. We asked the patient to join with us in prayer, if he (or she) could, while the musicians played.
>
> For many, prayer is a true liberation. At first we prayed for them across the bars of their bolted cells. But by the third week they were moving about freely in the patio. The fourth week they came of themselves and asked for prayer and holy water, and after two more weeks many were well enough to go home.
>
> The administrator and his team have been surprised to see peace descend upon the psychiatric hospital. The patients call our coming "happy Wednesday." By August 1981, there were only two patients who re-. mained in the hospital from the original group that we

had begun to visit. The rest had been released.

Other Recent Happenings

God's surprises continue, along with toil in his vineyard. The same parcel from Rick Thomas contained a sheaf of other reports. Among the highlights are the following:

The Multiplication of Lime. Manuel Basurto reports a multiplication of the lime which is used for plastering houses, May 7, 1981.

We were plastering a warehouse 140 feet long, 32 feet wide and 10 feet high. We had enough sand and cement but only 70 pounds of lime for plastering. We could not buy any because one man had bought it all. The construction foreman and I prayed and in faith went ahead with the plastering. After three days of plastering, the pile of lime had not gone down, even though we had used a lot. We continued to plaster and finished 72 feet of wall with the 70 pounds we had. Ordinarily, 70 pounds of lime would be enough for only 20 feet of wall. Moreover, the pile did not give out until the day when I was able to buy more lime in a hardware store in town. I believe the Lord wanted this multiplication because of the greed of the merchants who controlled the sale of lime.

Apples and Squash. Manuel Heredia and Juan Jaques report a multiplication of apples, October 15, 1979.

Likewise, Esther I. Padilla testifies to a multiplication of squash on the Lord's Ranch. "Normally, there were not enough to fill a potato sack, size 1001 B. Yet several sacks were filled to the top. This, despite the fact there was no indication that we had picked that many. . . ."

Water. Bill Halloran, engineer; Rick Thomas; Theresa Slavkosky; Rick Slavkosky; and Michael M. Halloran report a multiplication of water at the Lord's Ranch, August 18, 1979. Rick Thomas had given his neighbours permission to pump water with a centrifugal pump for a temporary operation that required a great quantity. They offered to pay but Rick said, "The water belongs to the Lord."

They filled a 500-gallon tank truck several times with a pump that delivered 830 gallons a minute. That should have created a water shortage. Instead, the water level did not even go down.

Other testimonies that arrived in the same parcel concerned multiplication of grapes at the Lord's Food Bank in July 1979 (testimony of Romelia Irrobali, and Martha Saldivar). There were also new testimonies regarding multiplications described earlier in this book, and testimonies relating to the cures of Rosa Maria Santos (August 1981) and Manny Basurto, in his own words (October 14, 1981).

Looking Back at Christmas 1972

Sister Mary Virginia writes about the first multiplication of food, Christmas 1972:

> When the two hostile groups of rubbish diggers had been reconciled, they gathered with us in such numbers that the food we brought was clearly not enough. We agreed to serve the children first, and then take care of the others as best we could. I said, "Don't worry. Everything will be all right."
>
> My heart told me: "God encouraged us to come to the Dump; he will not let us run short on the day of his birth." When the bags of tamales were dumped on the tables, I saw them bump together and become more. In

my heart I said to the Lord, "I knew that you would not let us down."

I watched as more bags were placed on the table, but the Lord said to me in my heart to let them be: it was his work not mine. Mine was to love the people and pray. Everything appeared normal to the human eye. Long lines of children received their food, and the grownups had a wonderful dinner together. It was the most beautiful Christmas dinner of my life.

Clearly, Christmas 1972 was not an accident, soon over and soon forgotten. God is faithful to those who are faithful to him. His power does not belong to the past nor to mythology. But today as yesterday, God needs men and women through whom he can reveal himself.

APPENDIX A

Cure: A Forgotten Gift

Cure is a much neglected topic in theology. There is no article on "cure" or "healing" in the *Dictionnaire de theologie catholique*, which comprises fifteen volumes and more than 40,000 columns. Why have the people of our century, Christians included, turned away from these gifts of God? There are many reasons.

   1. For a long time resignation prevailed over the (legitimate) desire to be cured.

   2. Asking God for this grace was thought improper because it seemed to be self-serving (when in fact one can ask to be healed or cured the better to serve others).

   3. This gift, it was felt, had come to an end. It was given for the foundation of the church, a sort of "honeymoon present," beyond which the church had long since passed.

   4. People were concerned, and rightly so, about tempting God and sinning by presumption, which is always a possibility.

   In more recent times, other considerations have contributed to the dismissal of cure or healing as a gift of God.

   5. There emerged the rationalist belief that healing or cure was the work of medical science and that the charismatic healings and cures of the past were a stopgap, pending the advent of modern medicine. In other words, healing or cure was directly ascribable to the medical treatment, a presumption abandoned by the medical profession itself, whose proper work is indeed to study the human body, its illnesses and how to treat them. To be healed or cured, on the other hand, is a process infinitely more subtle, complex, and mysterious. Already in the 16th century the French surgeon Ambroise Pare, quoting Ecclesiasticus, said: "I

doctored that man, but it was God who cured him."

6. People have also been cautioned against a wrong conception of God that would make him a sort of healer-magician. Rightly so, on condition that we do not forget that God heals.

7. Finally, the emphasis has been on medical verification, especially since the beginning of this century. But medical verification, instead of fulfilling its promise, has actually reached a sort of impasse for more reasons than one.

How God Cures

It is well that the charismatic renewal is not affected by these obstacles and has learned to trust again that cure and healing come from God. In order that this discovery, desired by God, remain sound and convincing, it is necessary to avoid any misdirection that might cast doubt or suspicion on the experience/phenomenon of cures. The renewal is aware of this, and the first step is to understand how and when God heals or cures. His ways are not always ours.

In essence, if God is good and generous, if he wants to cure, the cure is a free gift. Accordingly, the hope for cure must respect the mystery of God, whose plan and purpose does not always agree with our first desire. Bertrand Lepesant has described a case in point. A group felt pity for a crippled individual and stormed heaven for a cure. The forced prayer along with the command "Get up and walk"" failed. There was no cure. In fact, the crippled one himself did not desire it. He had come, looking for something other than to be healed of his glaring infirmity, something deeper, *first*. It was important that the group recognize the error that turned their pity into a desire for a cure that was not sensitive to God or to the crippled one himself.

Cure and Miracle

Physical cure does not necessarily involve miracle, in the sense of exception to the laws of nature. It is granted more often than miracle. It comes from a gift that is more interior. It is an overflow, a consequence of something not physical. The charismatic renewal has found that the infallible gift of grace (for anyone desiring it, and properly disposed) is healing from sin: in other words, conversion. That is the essential.

But conversion of the heart re-establishes and heals the authentic relationship with God and neighbour. It heals, at the same time, the relationship of the converted one to himself. Above all, it heals relationship with others (in the family and in society) and the relationships that are egotistic, warped, destructive. Normally, this healing from sin evolves into psychic healing. And that comes from a living fountain within us, the Holy Spirit. The fruits are hope and strength, joy and thankfulness, which radiate through the body and stimulate its health and defense mechanisms. For this reason, the process of physical healing or cure can be called, for want of a better word, *psychosomatic*, in the sense that this process operates at the juncture of body and mind (or spirit). But the word is only approximate and debatable as well.

The Extraordinary Case

Sometimes God goes further. He prolongs or accentuates in an extraordinary manner the process of irradiation, the action of the spiritual on the corporeal. He produces an unaccountable cure. It is then that we speak of miracle. The grace of God has accelerated or exceeded the ordinary processes.

This is a case for thanksgiving. But it is the exception and not what is most important. The important thing is not whether a cure was the most miraculous, the most extraordinary possible. The important thing is that the grace that heals one from sin penetrates the whole person, the psychical and physical nature.

I saw a beautiful illustration of this in the healing of a Japanese girl at Lourdes, in 1978. In her case no evidence was assembled and no verification process begun because she did not meet the criteria of "miracles." I informed her so by letter. She had been an invalid from birth, the consequence of an illness her mother had had during her pregnancy. She was unable to walk, and her deformities made it necessary to pile her bed with pillows. At Lourdes, returning from a procession of the Blessed Sacrament, she noticed some improvement. Her body, though not perfectly straight, showed signs of mending. The pillows became unnecessary. She learned to walk. She was still handicapped by the malformations of her body, but she could sleep in the normal position and walk by herself. Her attitude was this:

I thank God for having healed me. I thank him for having left me handicapped so that I could sympathize with my brothers and try to be of more help to them.

The blessing that the Lord had sent her was not only the relative cure but the grace to accept herself with thanksgiving and to use her restored powers to help other sick people. This was more beautiful and more impressive than a more miraculous cure of complete bodily restoration would have been. It also was more in conformity with the way of Christ as he faced the contradiction of the Cross. It is right to tell God of our desire to be made well the better to serve. But the fact is that one day we must die, any and all of us.

The healing and cures of this life are only a sign and annunciation of the Kingdom that is coming, the eternal Kingdom.

Hence, the important thing is to prefer God to the cure

that he gives, to begin by praising God, and to joyfully accept what he wills to give, as he wills to give it, in a spirit of complete hope, a hope which humbly includes the hope of cure.

The important thing, in other words, is to give everything its place:

The present life—an instant as it were, which the gospel wants us to live, but also its eternal dimension that does not pass away.

Nature—hygiene, medical recourse for specific diagnoses and therapies, which retain their role and honour, as the Book of Ecclesiasticus teaches:

> Honour the physician with the honour due him, according to your need of him, for the Lord created him; but healing comes from the Most High as a gift one receives from the king. . . . He gave skill to men that they might glory in his mighty works. (Eccl 28:1–6)

Prayer for healing does not make the physician's care unnecessary. It creates better relations with the physician because he is not expected to play God but simply to practice his science, his art, and his compassion.

God especially must be given his place. It is from him that we receive the love that heals. This is why a purely egoistic desire to be healed or the cultivation of autosuggestion is not the way to healing. The true way is to seek God's love first, to be disposed for whatever he wills and for whatever desire the Holy Spirit awakens, along with thanksgiving that God has given us what is best. In this approach we can thank him beforehand for the healing he wills to give, to help him give it. This is how the charismatic renewal prays, by beginning with God, with thanksgiving.

Does God Will to Heal?

There is no doubt that Christ willed to heal. Healings and

cures stand out in the gospel. They form the most numerous category of miracles. Jesus, who refused to give "signs from heaven," never refused a supplication for healing. He even solicits the supplication: "Do you want to be healed [*hygiano*]?" (Jn 5–6). He is pleased when he is asked to heal or cure. He expresses great joy when such healing is sought in great faith, including great confidence, in which case he grants it even more readily.

Healing, then, is a fact of the gospel, and one wonders why it is no longer clearly taken up in books of theology.

"Jesus went about . . . healing every disease and every infirmity," says Matthew (Mt 9:35). *"He went about . . . healing all that were oppressed by the devil,"* says Peter (Acts 10:38).

The charism of healing which he had as Son of God he exercised in a human way, at a distance in the case of the Centurion's servant, but more often by speaking with the sick person, placing his hands on the afflicted, performing unctions, even with his spittle. Humbly he brought his body into play. It is a fact, whatever one's interpretation.

Jesus did not keep this charism for himself, as an exclusive gift of which we only have nostalgic rememberance. He communicated it to his church.

He sent out the Twelve two by two to preach the Kingdom (the gospel) in the Palestinian villages (Mt 10:1–8; Mk 6:13; Lk 9: 2–6), and stressed the gift of healing he was giving them: *"Heal the sick, raise the dead, cleanse lepers, cast out demons,"* he said to them.

Luke alone relates another mission in which Jesus sends, not just the Twelve but seventy-two disciples two by two with the same instructions, not only of preaching and poverty (first) but of healing: *"Heal the sick . . . and say to them: The kingdom of God has come near to you"* (10:9).

In the last chapter of Mark, just before the ascension Jesus makes this promise to the disciples:

These signs will accompany those who believe: in my name they will cast out demons; they will speak in new tongues; they will pick up serpents . . . they will lay their hands on the sick and they will recover.

This is what we see happening in the Acts of the Apostles after the gift of the Holy Spirit has transformed, baptized in the Spirit, and strengthened these same apostles and disciples, who had fled during the Passion of Jesus.

We see the apostles working numerous healings, according to the mission and power that God had given them. The Acts of the Apostles singles out those of the two great apostles.

Peter. There was the lame man at the gate called Beautiful (Acts 3:1–11; cf. 4:14). After this healing, which brought on persecution, the apostles were confirmed by a new Pentecost (cf. Acts 4:31).

There was also Aeneas, the paralytic: "*Aeneas, Jesus Christ heals you; rise and make your bed*" (Acts 9:33).

Luke even says that the mere shadow of Peter produced healing (Acts 5:15:16).

Paul. At Lystra, Paul healed the cripple from birth who had never walked. "*Stand upright on your feet,*" Paul said to him, "*and he sprang up and walked*" (Acts 14:8–10).

At Malta, there was the father of Publius, sick with fever and dysentery and many others who then came and were cured (Acts 28:9).

Correspondingly for Paul: Luke says, God did extraordinary miracles by the hands of Paul, so that handkerchiefs or aprons were carried away from his body to the sick, and diseases left them and the evil spirits came out of them (Acts 19:12).

What is portrayed here is an exceptional profusion of the

charism, a bewildering use of the sign with a readiness that should not be overlooked.

Sometimes, as also shown here, an outpouring of confidence produces behaviour which, for the moment, seems extravagant. All the more reason, then, to beware lest these signs of God's gift be perceived as a sort of magic formula in which God is overlooked and the signs themselves are deprived of their divine character.

The Eucharist: Sacrament of Healing

First of all, to say that these gifts of healing were limited to Christ's public life is not true. Neither the Bible (Acts of the Apostles) nor the history of the church warrants such a conclusion. There has always been healing down through the centuries and, surprisingly, despite many excesses, the church has never condemned anyone engaged in healing. This is perhaps the only domain that has escaped condemnation, a remarkable fact in itself. The gift of Christ in the Eucharist is first of all the gift of himself for eternal life. This gift, however, manifests itself in strength and healing.

Second, the Eucharist is a sacrament of nourishment. Food is a sign, a bearer of *strength* and *growth* but also of healing. And it is a *remedy*, as indicated in the prayer of the Mass, just before Communion: "Lord Jesus Christ, with faith in your love and mercy I eat your body and drink your blood. Let it not bring me condemnation (cf. 1 Cor 11:29), *but health in mind and body.*"

This is what the liturgy teaches in the Mass. The healing asked for is spiritual, which does not exclude but implies bodily healing, if we have faith in it, if we seek it.

The alterntive prayer says more directly: "May your Body and Blood deliver me from all my sins and from *every evil*" [not only sin but every evil, including physical and psychical illness].

The last prayer before Communion is that of the

Centurion: "Lord, I am not worthy to receive you, but say only the word and I shall be healed."

In effect, the church calls on communicants to apply to themselves the words by which the Centurion besought the Lord to heal his son. The prayer refers in the first instance to the healing of the heart, interior healing to receive the Lord worthily, in all love, and so be healed even as to the body, in order to serve him better: healing from sin, plus psychical and physical healing.

Third, the Eucharist is the sacrament of the Body of Christ. It nurtures the unity of the Body, its harmony and strength. It fosters its growth. The Eucharist as substantial sacrament structures the church, the body of Christ, from within.

Finally, the eucharist is the sacrament of hope. In this sacrament we "proclaim the Lord's [victorious] death until he comes" (1 Cor 11:26). Beyond the daily bread, the Eucharist calls us to the eternal hope, to resurrection in Christ, to the salvation of our whole being that Jesus wants for us, body and soul.

We have seen, then, that the Eucharist is a fundamental source of healing. Much more could be said by way of specifics. But better to stay with what is most central and concentrate on the Person of Christ, source of healing, by himself and through the sign and reality of his Eucharist, principle of health and vitality in the church.

APPENDIX B

New Testament Vocabulary of Healing

It may be well to recall the variety of words used in the New Testament when speaking of healing.

1. *Hygiano*, whence our word hygiene, has the sense of return to health, to be made well (Mk 5:34; Jn 5:6,9; 7:23; Acts 4:10).

2. *Therapeuo*, whence our word therapeutic. Cf. Lk 9:11: Jesus brings health to those who had need of *therapeia* (healing or therapy).

3. *Iaomai*, from the Greek root which denotes physician *iatros*, as in English paed–iatrist. It is used in the nominative case when Christ is compared to a physician: "Those who are well have no need of a physician [*iatrou*, here equals Christ], but those who are sick" (Mk 2:17). The root sense also appears in St. Paul's designation for the charism of healing, *charisma iamaton* (1 Cor 12:9, 28, 30).

4. *Sozo*, to save, is also used in the sense of being healed: "If I touch even his garments, I shall be saved [made well]," said the woman with the flow of blood (Mk 5:28, 34; similarly in 5:23 for the daughter of Jairus; 6:56, all who touched the fringe of his garment were made well; 10:52, the blind beggar healed to whom Jesus said; "Your faith has saved you"; Lk 6:9; 7:3, 8, 36, 48, 50; 17:19, a leper; 18:42, a blind man).

5. *Katharizo*, to purify. Its root appears in the word *catharsis*, appropriated from the Greek and used typically in

psychiatric healing. A medieval heretical sect called themselves *Cathari*, the pure.

This word is used to indicate healing that eliminates the morbid elements responsible for illness, in the realm of sin, of mental and emotional life as well as in the body. It is used especially, and significantly, for the cure of lepers (Mt 8:2–3; 10:8, 11:5, the lepers are cleaned, i.e., cured of leprosy; Mk 1:40–44; Lk 4:27; 5:12–14; 7–22; 17:14–17, the ten lepers).

6. *Apolyo*, to loose from, set free, release. Used only in Lk 13:12, *Woman, you are freed from your infirmity* denotes healing as liberation or deliverance, which also is rich in meaning.

7. *Kompsoteros echo*, to be better (in health). In Jn 4:52 the official of Capernaum asks at what hour his child healed by Jesus *began to be better*.

8. *Kalos echo*, Jesus *placed his hands on the sick and they are well*.

The expression has a fine Hellenist flavor: literally to be *beautiful*, with the sense of being *well*. Greek loves to associate beautiful-and-well (*kalos k'agathos*). Yes, healing is beautiful, especially when it is a gift of the Lord.

APPENDIX C

What Is a Miracle?

Christianity, which "demythologized" God, not through rationalist criticism, but as a consequence of an encounter and an experience, has always oscillated between two attitudes in regard to miracle. Today, the extremes are represented on the one hand by certain Christians who regard miracle as unworthy of God and unacceptable to the scientific mind. Others, by contrast, are avid seekers of the marvelous and hope and believe they can meet God sometimes by way of the senses, direct, and transparent.

What, then, is a miracle? The definition now lodged in the minds of people and in dictionaries—*an exception to natural laws*—is relatively recent. The notion has a complex history.

The Bible makes no clear distinction between what conforms to the laws of nature and what is an exception to these laws. For the Bible all of creation is a wonder of God. It is admired in total as one grand miracle. Even the rainbow was part of the miracle. This fundamental conception was adopted by St. Augustine, who died in 430. For several centuries thereafter little thought was given to the boundaries between the natural and the supernatural (a word foreign to the Bible) or to the need for verifying phenomena specifically miraculous.

Names and Meaning

The diversity of words used in the New Testament for what we call miracle points to the complexity of the question and its obscurities.

Four terms are used in the New Testament:

1. *Sign*: Greek *semeion*, Hebrew *otot*.
2. *Prodigy*: Greek *teras*, Hebrew *moftin*.
3. *Marvel*: Greek *thauma*.
4. *Glory*: Greek *doxa, endoxa, paradoxa*.

These first two terms bring to mind the whole discussion over miracle and the divergent views it has evoked. Is miracle a sign that speaks of God? Or is it a prodigy, a reversal of the laws of nature? The New Testament often uses these two names together (sixteen times, to be exact). For the believer, the more important term must surely be *sign*. Miracle is of interest as an expression of God and especially as an expression of Christ, indicating the faith and portal of salvation that God offers to man. In this respect, miracle differs from magic, with its accent on prodigy.

It is not immaterial, however, that a sign has a prodigious or exceptional character and thereby manifests God's transcendence and his free grace.

In New Testament usage, therefore, these two terms are not opposed to each other, the second (prodigy) being considered less as a fracture of laws with a materiality of its own, and more as the attestation of God's power and his interest in man. Only later did the emphasis shift to prodigy as argument for the truth of Revelation, whose object is not evident: *a stumbling block to Jews, foolishness to pagans*. Thus, when their faith is challenged, Christians have often cited miracles as a signature of God and of Christ. This argument appears as early as Origen, who distinguishes the miracles of Christ from magical phenomena by their religious purpose, "because they are given for the salvation of souls, the reform of morals and the repute of Christian worship." Arnobius adds that magicians cannot do the one-thousandth part of what Christ did (*Adversus Nationes*, 1, 43, *PL* 5, 779).

The word miracle, which prevails in our language, derives from the Latin *miraculum*, a wonder, a marvel, and from the verb *mirari*, to wonder, to be astonished at.

The New Testament does not use this term formally, or as an independent name. The gospels do underline the admiration, the amazement of the crowd in seeing the works of Christ or God, but the Greek word *thauma* (a marvel that causes wonder) is not used as a formal designation of miracle but only to qualify it. (Luke uses two analogous terms, once each, to designate the wonders wrought by Christ: *endoxa*, in Lk 13:17 and *paradoxa*, in Lk 5:2, the paradoxes of God. The Greek word *doxa* (glory) signifies and connotes that it is a question of *glorious* works.)

For a long time prophecies were regarded as more wonderful miracles than healings or cures.

St. Augustine is the first to give an express definition of miracle in the very large sense spoken of above. But he distinguishes two categories: (1) daily miracles, perceptible in the natural course of events and (2) a more restrictive sense which incorporates the other aspect of the gospel vocabulary, prodigy:

> I call miracle that which is hard to bring about (*arduum*) or is out of the ordinary, such as exceeds the expectation or capability of the one who marvels (*miratur: De utilitate credendi 16, 34, PL 32, 90*).

He sees in this unwonted character the criterion of a special intervention by God.

St. Gregory directs attention to the first category of miracles: the daily birth of people who did not exist is more wondrous than the raising of a dead person who had already been alive; and the multiplication of bread is less wondrous than the harvest from a grain of wheat sown in the ground and dying. But because of their habitual character these daily wonders pale. What happens every day, however marvelous, is diminished by familiarity (*quotidiana vilescunt: Moralia 4, 15–18, PL 75, 738–739*).

The Middle Ages took a more analytical approach to the

question of miracles. Generally speaking, they took over the Augustinian conception but with developments of their own.

St. Anselm was the first to make an analysis on the basis of three causes: nature, the free will of man, and the will of God. Miracle derived from the third cause, intervention by God.

In line with this was William of Auxerre's definition of miracle as *super-natural*, that which is *above* nature (*supra-naturam*) as compared with natural occurrences, which are *according to* nature (*secundum naturam*).

St. Thomas Aquinas distinguishes three aspects of miracle: (1) It is out of the ordinary (as in the second meaning of St. Augustine); (2) it upsets the natural order, being *above* or *outside* of what could be expected of nature; (3) but most of all, miracle for him is what cannot be brought about except by God.

He reduces the three aspects to this definition:

> "Miracle is what fills with wonder (*admiratione plenum*), whose cause is absolutely hidden from us, namely God, and that is why miracle is said to be what God produces beyond causes known to us."

He goes on to say that miracle is an exception to the natural order of creation (*praeter naturam*). He would be more reserved on the modern notion of a divine intervention *contrary to nature* which theologians are increasingly inclined to regard as inconsistent with God's wisdom.

Modern Critique of Miracle

Essentially, the old analyses of miracle confined themselves to what was found in the biblical narrative, interpreted in the most literal way. Since then, two cultural facts have changed the nature of the problem. In other words, science was born, and what gave it birth were two insistent and simultaneous compulsions.

1. One was the postulate of determinism, which conceived the universe as an unfailing chain of explicable facts, a universe that left no place for supernatural (extra-natural) interferences. Science arose out of this postulate, which scored its triumph. In the 16th century, physicians in robes and peaked hats still classified the causes of diseases as *physical* or moral (venereal disease being considered punishment for sexual transgressions), natural or supernatural, diabolical or divine. Science began when the researcher in the laboratory excluded every appeal to non-observable causes *and refused to declare anything inexplicable, on the ground that science does not capitulate to the inexplicable but continues to look for an explanation until it finds one.*

This postulate excludes God's intervention in the world. But it is only a postulate. It has been confirmed by success. It has not been proven. There could be a place for a non-determinist science, just as there is for non-Euclidean geometries.

Modern theologians generally adhere to determinism. Their reason for accepting it is that God would not violate the order he has established. They find additional support in the classical teaching that God does not act like second causes but in a transcendent manner (not accessible to observation), which is embodied in a normal play of second causes, the area where the postulate of determinism applies.

2. But science is not only rational; it is also experimental. It affirms nothing except on experience, repeatable and verifiable. Miracle does not lend itself to such control, since it is essentially an unpredictable, free gift of God.

Believers have often disputed determinism but have generally accepted the experimental role of science. They have availed themselves of it in the authentication of miracles. In the 18th century Cardinal Prosper Lambertini

(Benedict XIV) drew up norms of their verification for the process of canonization. Popular enthusiasm for saints or rumored saints threatened to get out of hand. Veneration often was premature and inspired by equivocal evidence (reputation for holiness, preservation of the body, alleged miracles at the graveside). Rigorous control was called for.

By the beginning of our century, authentications of miracle had assumed exclusive importance, so as to over-shadow *the miracle itself.* Faced with rationalism, which denied the possibility of any miracle, believers sought to prove that there were miracles which no laws of nature could explain, and if so, scientism would be vanquished on its own ground. "One solidly proven miracle is enough to destroy the system," it was said.

This was the general attitude when, in 1905, the Bureau of Medical Verifications was established at Lourdes on the advice of Pius X. Its purpose was both to sift our illusory claims (whether stemming from credulity or hysteria) and to present to believers' solid cases duly attested and recognized, in order to refute anticlerical adversaries.

The Bureau got off to a good start. From 1907 to 1913, thirty-three miraculous healings and cures were recognized.

Authentications came to a halt with the First World War and were resumed after the Second, in 1946. Bishop Theas restructured the process. He created a Medical Bureau at Lourdes charged with examining case histories and an International Medical Commission composed of top medical authorities, whose task it is to pass final judgment on the scientific level.

Verification of Miracle

To the medical doctors of this Commission the church poses three questions:

1. Was there sickness (and what kind)?

2. Was there cure, complete, instantaneous, etc.?

3. Was the cure or healing inexplicable by science?

In answering the first two questions, doctors are on home ground. But the third one disturbs them, because it is of the nature of medicine, as of science, to deny the inexplicable and to seek without apology a scientific explanation. Saying that a cure is inexplicable would be tantamount to renouncing the postulate from which all science proceeds. That is why the doctors usually respond by adding the clause: inexplicable *in the present state of science*.

But this confuses the issue and leaves it hanging. According to the *juridical* norms set up by Rome, such a restriction voids the testimony of medicine. It is, in fact, an escape clause. And it constitutes a problem that is not yet resolved.

Today, scientism and anti-scientism have been superseded by a new order of science, less sure of itself, more penetrated with the complexity of reality and conscious of its inability to draw conclusion except in terms of relativity, probability, statistical analysis, and so forth.

For the believer it is not a question of subduing scientism with its excessive pretensions, in the name of equally excessive pretensions that promise strict proof of miracle, whereas Christ himself did not restrain the freedom of his adversaries and did not submit to their tests when they asked a sign from heaven.

The purpose of the scientific consultation instituted by the church should be to make a medical evaluation of the astonishing cases in which the believer sees an encounter and intervention of God. This scientific evaluation, however, can only be in terms of probability. Yet probability would be in line with theological demands as well as those of science, since God's intervention in the world is truly mysterious. It is not an object of geometric proof but only of a kind of conjectural discernment whose certitude cannot be communicated because it derives from a personal, interior light given to the believer.

At once clear and obscure, the miraculous always leaves a way out for those so inclined. It is sometimes said that a miracle never grew back an arm or leg. Perhaps this is impossible, but if it did happen, one would probably have to "tell it to the marines." The scientific attitude, in any case, would be to look for an explanation.

The rules in effect today for the verification of miracles clearly need to be revised. The standard question of *whether a cure or healing was inexplicable* might well be replaced with another: In what way was this cure or healing out of the ordinary, at odds with prognosis, with common experience, and the known laws of medicine? This procedure would permit a better assessment of these phenomena and also make it possible to study them with an objectivity and serenity more appropriate to both faith and science.

Their verification remains difficult in any event, because miracle is not a normal object of experience. Whatever its nature, it is the work of God's special intervention, a free gift not experimentally repeatable. Which is to say, it cannot be tested out in a laboratory. But the procedures of probability "familiar to science" could be applied to many cases, at Lourdes and elsewhere.

Perplexity of the Church in the '60s

It should be emphasized that the church has never asked the medical profession as such to *certify any miracle*. The three questions posed to doctors with a view to authentication do not contain the word *miracle*. They only ask for a technical and scientific opinion on a given fact of healing. Authentication, the formal judgment that a cure or healing was miraculous, devolves on the bishop of the diocese to which the cured or healed person belongs. Upon receiving the medical statement, which is a preliminary step, an

ommission studies the religious context of the
in question, its moral and spiritual fruits, for
uals and communities, for the previously sick one
e entourage. These are the signs by which God's work
in the life of his people is recognized.

The church, which sometimes lags behind a revolution,
has gone through a period of perplexity over the question of
miracles, particularly in recent times as new circumstances
of faith and science arose. Meanwhile, seemingly miraculous occurrences did not cease. Yet the church has been so
beset with indecision that responsible authorities sometimes
chose to suppress these occurrences rather than declare
themselves.

At Lourdes no certification of miracles happened for
more than ten years, from 1965 to 1977. The sick who made
pilgrimage to the shrine were expressly told not to noise it
abroad if they were healed until the healings had been duly
certified. This meant a waiting period that kept getting
longer and longer, as many as twelve years and more.

Even in cases where doctors, speaking as doctors,
acknowledged a cure, the bishop of the miracle might
"classify" the case. Or he might have it examined by a
commission which, forgetting its proper competence
(religious), would reopen the medical inquiry already
closed by the International Committee and sometimes vote
in the negative on the word of a local doctor or psycho-
analyst.

Medical findings assumed such importance that the
ecclesiastics began to view them as the sole criterion and
became preoccupied with them instead of doing their own
work (that of identifying the moral and spiritual circumstances), or if they adhered to their task, performed it
according to criteria that were purely institutional and
juridic. So, for example, one of the most remarkable cures
of these latter years was set aside by the bishop because the
person involved was a divorcee. Is God forbidden to work a

miracle for a divorcee? And, assuming that C҉
to such a person, would it not be worth th҉
inquire what happened as a consequence, rath҉
changing to a juridicism that forgets the words of C҉
"The Sabbath was made for man and not man for th҉
Sabbath"?

At Lourdes, at the present time, these paradoxes and
anomalies are being overcome. The ecclesiastical represent-
atives are beginning to rise above the lingering rationalism
that had taken hold from 1965–1975. Recently, two case
histories of a miraculous nature that had been held up were
recognized: one from Italy (V. Micheli, cured in June 1963,
recognized fourteen years later; in 1977); and a more recent
case from Anger in France, that of Serge Perrin, accountant:
victim of "chronic, organic hemiplegia with ocular lesions
brought on by cerebral circulatory problems; no effective
treatment known, instant cure, no relapses."

This latter cure, in April 1970, was confirmed by the
International Medical Commission on October 17, 1976,
and recognized by the bishop of Anger in June 1978.
Previous cases had led to the suspicion that he would not
recognize it, and his recognition of it as miraculous was a
surprise.

In our time science has become more modest and more
aware of the complexity of reality, which the human mind
can never exhaust. In this respect we are closer to St.
Augustine than to the simplistic ideology imposed by
scientism even on believers and non-believers alike: the
doctrine of a network of causes reducible to a single
formulation, an all-inclusive principle. Believers rallying to
the defense of miracles, felt compelled to show how God
could break the laws he had established—like the watchmaker changing the hands of his watch, more or less. The
better the watchmaker, the less he has to tinker with his
watches. This raises a question as to the nature of miracle.
Does God produce this sign of his presence as a contra-

diction of science or as a manifestation for the community of believers? The second interpretation tends to prevail.

Significance and Future of Miracles

A miracle is not an arbitrary demonstration of God's omnipotence, whose basic character is its incompatibility with the laws of nature. Miracles belong to the universal context of salvational history. They are part of the process by which God gives himself to man, freely, gratuitously. These external signs accredit God's messengers. They are also a pledge of the future.

Will this more comprehensive understanding bring an end to the phenomena of rejection that have plagued the Church in these latter years? Will it permit a return to the teaching of Vatican Council I (1870), which condemned as anathema those who declare miracles impossible and relegate them to fable and myth?

In 1958, Professor Mauriac (brother of François Mauriac) said:

—I believe, not because of miracles but in spite of them.

This remark conveys the sincere attitude of most Christian intellectuals. At the time, the Holy Office dispatched emissaries to Dr. Mauriac and several others, with a polite request to amend the wording of their report before publication. The corrections obtained masked the problem rather than resolving it.

These difficulties are beginning to be met. The solution lies essentially in the revision of a naive concept of miracle and a naive concept of science. Scientism and antiscientism, polemical ideologies, fed on each other and were doomed to the same death, like clericalism and anticlericalism. Their demise was long overdue. A new sensitivity to God's perspective developed, one that promises a more just view of his working in the world around us.

Bibliographical note on details on the miracles of Lourdes: B. Billet and Dr. Olivieri, *Y a-t-il encore des miracles à Lourdes?* Paris, Lethielleux, 4th edition, 1979 (revised by Dr. Mangiapan, president of the Medical Bureau). On the basic questions of miracle: R. Laurentin, *Catholic Pentecostalism,* Garden City, New York, Doubleday, 1977, pp. 123–131, and *Lourdes, pelerinage pour notre temps,* Paris, Chalet, 1977, pp. 112–128.

*　　*　　*

Notes

1. Speaking in tongues: a prayer of inspired praise, usually in mysterious language, the nature of which is much debated.

2. That was in 1975, April 10th to be precise. He has worked at the Dump since October 4th, 1975.

3. Father Thomas' city is underway. At the beginning of 1981, a well had been dug and three houses and two warehouses put up.

*　　*　　*

Fr. René Laurentin is a French theologian and journalist whose major books include *Catholic Pentecostalism* and *Bernadette of Lourdes*. He is a regular contributor to *Le Figaro* and *Paris Match*.